MODERN LEADER

MODERN LEADER

JeVON McCORMICK

LIONCREST
PUBLISHING

MODERN LEADER

FIRST EDITION

ISBN   978-1-5445-3228-8 *Hardcover*
      978-1-5445-3227-1 *Ebook*
      978-1-5445-3229-5 *Audiobook*

TO ALL WHO HAVE NEVER FELT
ACCEPTED, NEVER BELONGED, AND
NEVER FIT THE PLAYBOOK...

WELCOME.

CONTENTS

FOREWORD

SOME OF YOU MAY KNOW WHO I AM ALREADY, BUT I KNOW
there are many of you who may not, especially coming from
the business world. My name is David Goggins. I'm a retired
Navy SEAL, an endurance athlete, and the *New York Times*
Bestselling author of *Can't Hurt Me*.

I did twenty-one years in the military. I've seen many "leaders".
Most of those leaders were actually managers who never truly
understood what it meant to lead.

Being a leader requires so much more than most people think.
It's not about making sure people punch a clock. It requires a
dedication to service, and a commitment to yourself that you
will set the standard to guide others. Our world has too few true
leaders right now. JT McCormick is one of them.

Mindset and leadership are forged through adversity. JT was born into a life where becoming a Modern Leader wasn't just a choice, it was his only option. JT told this story in his first book, *I Got There*. Reading about where he came from and what he went through, it would be easy to see how he could have ended up just another statistic. There is no MBA program that will teach you what JT's life taught him—I know that from firsthand experience.

For most of my life, I walked a hard road. And while JT's story is not exactly like mine, there are many similarities between us. The biggest similarity is the work he had to put in to get him to where he is now. If there is one thing I understand, it's how daunting that task had to have been. When you are "the only one" in any group, it's difficult to even get in the game, let alone rise to the top.

I've been referring to JeVon as JT, and that's on purpose. As you read *Modern Leader*, you'll come to know the story of JeVon's name and sacrifice of his identity that ran parallel to his rise in business. He decided to share this story with me a year ago. It truly touched me; understanding the lessons he learned to survive at a young age makes the evolution he has made as a man and a leader even more resonant.

Our world is changing so rapidly that it requires new and different teachers. You can't come from one slice of life and have all the answers anymore; we need teachers who have experienced a little bit of everything. JeVons are not a dime a dozen, and the knowledge they offer is priceless.

If you feel called to lead, the dedication required is something that you can't learn from just anyone. Few people are qualified to teach that course. I'm here to tell you that JeVon McCormick is more than qualified, and the insights he shares in this book will change how you view leadership.

—DAVID GOGGINS, RETIRED NAVY SEAL, ULTRAMARATHONER AND TRIATHLETE, SPEAKER, AND AUTHOR OF *CAN'T HURT ME*

A TIME FOR ACTION

"I'm frustrated."

The room was silent.

Everyone in the conference room and on the large TV where our video call was displayed stared back at me. No one spoke. For a moment, it felt like no one *breathed*. All eyes were on me, waiting for my next word.

I've had enough practice in front of large audiences to know the rhythms of a good speech. I can feel when to pause, when to speak faster, and when to build volume to move the crowd.

I know when to back off and when to push forward. A good speech is like music. I know when I have the audience's attention—and I know how to hold it.

That day, I had their attention. But this was different from all the speeches I've given and all the other meetings I've led. That day, speaking into the microphone to all the people who make up the company I serve as CEO, I wasn't performing.

I wasn't the polished CEO delivering a rousing speech to rally the company. I wasn't the business leader up onstage at a conference giving a keynote.

I wasn't JT.

For the first time in front of these people, I was JeVon.

I took a deep breath and continued.

"All I can do is speak to you from the heart, and be vulnerable with you. You've asked me how I feel. The answer is that I'm frustrated. I'm extremely frustrated. Because *this is not new*."

The week before, all of us in the room and the entire country had watched an event unfold that had changed everything. For many, it was the first time they'd seen anything like it. But for some of us, it was chillingly familiar.

Another unarmed black man had been killed in police custody. One of hundreds, thousands since I've been alive.

The only difference with what happened to George Floyd is that this time, someone filmed it. This time, we all watched a video of a white police officer kneeling on a black man's neck until he died.

It was not new.

Yet the world reacted like it was the first time it had ever happened.

Looking back on it now, I can see how the country was primed for the outpouring of shock, rage, and grief that followed George Floyd's murder.

May 2020 and the months leading up to it had been a bonfire of stress. In January, we'd started seeing the news reports of a virus that was shutting down whole countries across the world. By February, cases were mounting in the United States. Hospitals everywhere were ringing the alarm. People were getting afraid.

And by March, we were locked down.

Like every CEO, I've faced tough times. I've had to let people go. I've navigated organizational chaos that seemed like it would never be untangled. I've even stayed the course while facing a bank balance that required me to personally make payroll.

But this was different. The virus disruption was hands down the most stressful challenge I've ever encountered.

As businesses everywhere sent their employees home in March, layoffs began sweeping through the American workplace almost as rapidly as the virus itself. It reminded me of 2008, when I had been working in the mortgage industry. I remembered what it was like to lay off entire departments. I remembered how all those people had families to support, bills to pay, and careers that evaporated.

These memories hit me hard every day in March 2020 as I watched our company Slack light up with photos of newborns. Several people in our company had just moved across the country to Texas to come work with Scribe. The day before I made the decision to shut the office down on March 15th, someone had posted a photo of the house they'd worked hard to purchase as a first-time homeowner.

Scribe's executive team wasn't getting how serious the situation was. One day soon after we closed the office in March, I lost my cool on them in a video meeting.

"You don't understand," I shouted, which is rare for me. "You all don't know what it was like to lay people off back in 2008. I was there. I remember."

My emotional state mirrored that of the world at the time. The future was more uncertain than ever before. Fear, anxiety, confusion, stress, anger; it was all boiling under the surface, and George Floyd's death tipped the balance.

As the weeks unfolded, I watched. I watched as people protested all over the country. I watched as some of those protests became riots, explosions of violence that I could not condone.

I watched as businesses started to realize that unlike most things in our one-hour news cycle, this outcry wasn't going away. I watched as CEOs, boardrooms, and PR heads scrambled to respond.

And as I watched the response of business leadership across the country, I got frustrated.

Empty statement after empty statement. Token commitments to "DEI". Pulling Aunt Jemima off the shelves of supermarkets. Blackout Tuesday on social media.

What does posting a black square on your company Instagram actually *do* for racial injustice? What change is that going to bring about?

These gestures struck me as shallow, trivial, even cynical. I watched in mounting frustration as the gestures themselves became the conversation. Companies congratulated each other for "action", when all I saw was talk. The same talk I've always heard.

"I'm frustrated," I told the room that day at Scribe. "Did we really wake up as a country because we watched a murder take place live on video? I don't know. I hear people say that this time it *feels* different. To me, it doesn't. I hear people saying how sad it is that a man passed away while saying, 'I can't breathe.' I have to ask, *which one?*"

Like every speech, I was building a rhythm. The audience was with me. When I paused, not a sound could be heard in the room—except my own heartbeat pounding in my ears.

I wasn't nervous. I was frustrated. Frustrated with all the talk. Frustrated with the superficial gestures. Frustrated with the declarations of change that always went nowhere, that led us to exactly the same place we'd been so many times before.

Growing up on welfare in economically depressed Dayton, Ohio taught me that talk means nothing. Talk doesn't get you off the streets. Talk doesn't put food on the table. Talk doesn't get the JeVons of the world off the street and into the boardroom.

A leader's responsibility is to take *action*, and what I saw in the summer of 2020 was a total failure of leadership.

It wasn't new.

This book is about how we can change that together.

AN EVOLUTION OF LEADERSHIP

Something isn't working.

Everywhere we turn, we're surrounded by evidence that leadership is failing: civil unrest, political tribalism, cancel culture, corporate apologies. Even movements like Black

Lives Matter and #metoo signal a collective release of anger and frustration.

People feel let down. They feel abandoned. Leaders are failing to lead.

Why?

Is it really a simple case of leaders falling asleep at the wheel? Is it just that they aren't trying hard enough? Is it that they don't care enough?

I hear all the time that most executives truly don't care about anything but profit. That their decisions and actions are focused on fattening the bottom line, and have nothing to do with the well-being of the people actually doing the work. That any attempt at a people-first initiative is a hollow gesture designed to make the company look good, without really having much impact on the people it's supposed to serve.

I can see that argument ringing true in the past, but not today. That's not what I see.

When I spend time with CEOs, executives, and business leaders, I see people who agree that there's a problem. They're aware of a creeping sense of distrust and dissatisfaction. They can see the destabilizing effect of each new disruption. Some of them are even doing the work to find solutions; they're trying things, but nothing is working.

They can see that there's a hole in their game. They're missing something, but they don't know what.

As business leaders, I wrote this book for you.

The problems we face today are unique to this moment. There are certainly lessons we can draw from past leaders, and in this book, I'll highlight some of my favorites. But leaders of the past were running an old playbook—and for the modern problems we face today, that playbook won't work.

Modern problems demand modern solutions.

This moment demands a Modern Leader.

Modern Leadership is a new way of serving in business. The Modern Leader is equipped to lead for the future, not the past.

In this book, I've chosen to focus specifically on business leadership, even though obviously governments, nonprofits, and community leadership play a huge role in the direction of our society. Do I have opinions on where we've gone wrong politically in this country? *Yes*. More than my wife and friends probably want to hear about.

But that's not my world. I'm not a politics guy. I'm a business guy. I've devoted my life to studying, building, and leading businesses. What I've seen in the past decade, as leadership in every facet of US society has missed the mark, is that the greatest potential for leadership lies in business. Business is where we come together to create the future.

And up until now, we've all been working within a business landscape that leaves too many people out.

In bringing people together in business, we've been trained to look through a narrow lens. The people who make it into the room represent a small and nearly uniform slice of perspective and experience. With the same backgrounds, everyone tends to think the same. They tend to approach problems from the same angle. They drive solutions in the same direction.

What are we missing out on? How much greater could we be? How much more impact could your business make in the world if the people behind it represented a wider background of experience and perspective?

How much more profit could your business earn?

Yes, I said it: *profit*. I've noticed that whenever profit comes up in business, it's assumed that any effort that drives profit is in direct contradiction to any effort that supports people. We've placed profit and people on opposite ends of a dichotomy. The result is that you can't talk about prioritizing profit without raising the suggestion that you're *deprioritizing* people.

I call bullshit on that dichotomy.

I believe that people and profit are mutually enhancing. What's good for one is good for the other. There's no reason why serving people should diminish profit, and vice versa.

The old playbook is based partly on that false dichotomy. The old playbook says that if profit comes first, people come last.

In today's world, it's clear that that's not true. It's been proven time and time again that the more money, time, attention, and effort a company spends on ensuring the safety and well-being of its people, the higher that company's productivity, innovation, and profits rise.

But taking care of the people already in the room isn't where the action stops. The Modern Leader looks around at the people they serve and asks: *Who isn't in the room? Why? And how can I bring them in?*

The Modern Leader understands that without a broadening of perspective, their business is at risk. They understand that there is a whole world of people outside the narrow slice selected by the old playbook. The Modern Leader knows that their responsibility is to open their eyes to see everyone on the edges, open the door to invite them in, and then enable them to reach their greatest potential.

THE PLAYBOOK IS PLAYED OUT

Let's talk about the playbook our society has been running for hundreds of years. Finding success in business looks something like this:

You're born to a two-parent, middle-class or upper-class household. From the moment you're born, you have opportunities, and you have everything you need to take advantage of those opportunities. You have food on the table every night. You have books, music, the latest technology, and clothes that signal your status. You go to a school that prepares you for college. You have tutors who ensure you'll be accepted at a top school. You have parents who went to college, so right out of the gate, you're a legacy at at least two universities. You have money for college tuition, or even if you don't, you have the benefit of employed parents with a credit history who can cosign your student loans.

Running this playbook, a few things are relatively certain. Most likely, you're going to get a college degree. When you do, you're going to become part of a network of educated graduates who trade career advice, job postings, and contacts. You're going to see opportunities come your way.

This playbook, and every play you've been running your entire life, lead to one moment: the moment when your resume comes across a hiring manager's desk.

They pick up a well-designed piece of paper with a name at the top that they most likely recognize. Not because they know you—but because they know your *name*.

They've seen it before. It's a "safe" name. It's one of the hundreds of names that signals to the world what playbook your life has been running.

In case you were wondering, JeVon is *not* one of those names.

The hiring manager looks at your resume and considers your background, your experience, and your education. The conscious action is legitimate consideration; they're assessing your fitness for a role at the company.

The unconscious action, however, is a single thought: *This is a safe bet*.

They put you through to the next round.

Every day at companies across the country, this scene plays out like clockwork. Candidates become entry-level hires; entry-level hires rise through the ranks and take on leadership roles. Over time, the fabric of the company is subtly woven from the playbook that put each person there in the first place. The playbook's value is invisibly reinforced over and over again. It works. It's proven.

But without realizing it, companies have built themselves on shaky ground.

By running the old playbook, they've selected for a narrow

slice of experience and perspective. The risk of their position is hidden behind the harmony of everyone speaking the same language, understanding the same customs. The business *seems* strong, because everyone is on the same page. But then a disruption comes along, and they're left scrambling. What's more, each new disruption hits them harder than the last.

They can't figure out why. They can't see what they're missing.

What they're missing is this: the playbook that our society has been running for centuries is played out. It's already left most companies behind. Those who haven't realized it yet will be outmatched in the next decade, and likely won't last much longer than that.

So, as a business leader, what do you do?

As the President and CEO of a publishing company, I'm surrounded by books—not just the ones our company has helped create, but a whole universe of thought leadership and business writing. I see titles come across my desk constantly. And when you're around books as much as I am, you start to notice patterns.

These days, half the business books I see have the word "playbook" in the title somewhere. Everyone wants to win, and they're searching for the next play to run. Everyone's looking for a book that will tell them what to do.

When did *leaders* become *followers?*

If you're looking for a playbook, you won't find it here.

This book isn't a playbook. *Because leadership isn't a game.*

A TIME FOR ACTION

When it comes to the old playbook, my life couldn't have started further off the page.

I was born to a black pimp father who had twenty-three other children, and a white orphan mother. I grew up mixed-race in the deepest of poverty. I experienced racism, violence, abuse, assault, and homelessness on a constant basis.

I wrote about how I rose out of that circumstance and became successful in business in my book *I Got There.* It's the origin story of JT McCormick, whose race, education, and background weren't immediately obvious on the page—the kind of "safe bet" that got into the room.

Once I was in the room, I worked my way to the top.

But getting there in the first place? To do that, I had to run the old playbook.

Thirty years later in June of 2020, standing in front of the entire company I lead and speaking to them about my frustration, I was in a position I could barely imagine as a kid: privilege. I had created that privilege for myself instead of being born into it, but it was privilege all the same.

I had a platform and an audience. I was the President and CEO of a successful, rapidly growing company. I'd built tens of millions in personal wealth. I'd worked hard for nearly three decades to be standing where I was.

I got there—but in order to do so, I'd had to edit myself. My past. My story. My name.

JT got there. Not JeVon.

I was frustrated. I was tired of all the talk, tired of all the empty gestures. I wanted to see *action*.

So I made a choice.

That day speaking to our company was the last speech JT ever gave.

That day, for the first time, the business world heard JeVon speak.

I wrote *Modern Leader* because of that moment. I wrote this book to turn talk into action.

My goal is to offer a new leadership mindset and a look at a new business future, one based on optimism and openness, not the exclusionary rhetoric that's infused our society. The old playbook has left too many people behind already. It's time to create a new landscape that brings us all together—all the current leaders who fear irrelevance and are clinging to the ways of the past, and all the JeVons on the edges of our narrow view, waiting for their chance to speak.

DON'T READ THIS BOOK

Before you dive into Chapter 1, do me a favor.

Don't read this book unless you're willing to evolve.

This is a time for action. Don't read this book if you're not ready to take action.

This is a time for responsibility. If you're not going to finish this book, don't start it.

Don't read this book if you believe your current leadership strategy is working for you, and you have no interest in changing it.

If you treat diversity as a campaign or initiative, don't read this book.

If you're just looking to make your company look good, don't read this book.

Modern Leadership isn't a set of rules. What I'm offering in this book isn't a framework, guide, or instruction manual. Instead, what you'll read in this book is a way of thinking about your business that's focused on people and puts them first.

It sounds big, and if you've felt paralyzed by the scope of the problem, you don't have to be. Part of why I believe we've made so little progress in building a more inclusive business world is that people think they have to solve everything all at once. That's impossible. (And if a problem this big *could* be solved overnight, I have to believe we would have done it already.)

Taking your business into the future by evolving into Modern Leadership won't cost millions of dollars. In fact, it won't cost much more than intention, time, and willingness.

Willingness to open your eyes to the limitations of the old, broken playbook.

Willingness to open your doors to show people what's possible.

Willingness to open a backpack, to offer people the tools they need to be successful.

You'll read a lot of my story in this book, because that's what I have to bring to the table. I don't have all the answers. I don't have a degree from a top business school. In fact, I don't have a degree at all; I have a GED. I also have a perspective I haven't seen represented very often in business. Growing up mixed race, I was on the outside looking in most of the time; black people thought I was too white, and white people certainly didn't see me as one of them. As I climbed my way up in the business world, I came across room after room I wasn't welcomed into. To get inside, I had to figure out how to play the game. To be seen, I had to become someone else. I had to learn the playbook.

That's my story, but it doesn't have to be the next generation's story. Looking back now, I have a responsibility to all the JeVons who can't see what's possible for them. It wasn't my fault that I had to run the old playbook to get into the room, but now that I'm in it, it's my responsibility to expand the room, and welcome the future JeVons in.

That's Modern Leadership in a nutshell. The Modern Leader understands it may not be their *fault*, but it's their *responsibility*.

Above all, Modern Leadership is about people. *All* people. You, me, and everyone we'll see when we open our eyes.

If you're not willing to do that, then please: don't read this book.

If you are, then from this moment on, you are a Modern Leader.

Part One

OPEN YOUR EYES

CHAPTER 1

MY NAME IS JEVON

IT WASN'T UNTIL 1967 THAT I WAS "ALLOWED" TO BE BORN.

That's right—before the US Supreme Court handed down their decision in *Loving v Virginia* in June of 1967, my black father and white mother would have been committing a felony in most states by being together. I didn't come along until September of 1971, so I enjoyed a comfortable four-year distance from being born a crime.

When I think about how recent some of the darker moments of our history are, it makes me less surprised that we're still in such an angry, challenging place with race relations in this country. After all, laws like the one that would have prevented me from existing were around within the lifetimes of many people I know—and many business leaders who are in their fifties and older can remember a time when the idea of a JeVon in the boardroom was ridiculous.

When I reclaimed that name after decades of going by JT, my aim was to make JeVon just as "normal" in the boardroom as Steve, Tim, or Blake.

Thirty years ago, the name JT wasn't born out of fear or uncertainty, but a cold slap of reality. When I first started out in my career, trying to get in the door was more like banging my head against a wall. At the age of twenty-one, I was eager and had a work ethic no one could touch. I might have been outmatched on credentials by the business school grads who'd been running the old playbook their whole lives, but *no one* could outwork me. I was confident that hard work would eventually pay off.

But there was a problem I kept running into: I wasn't booking meetings or getting many callbacks. JeVon McCormick could cold call and follow up as many times as he wanted, but nobody was willing to listen.

Meanwhile, my white colleagues' phones rang off the hook, and their appointment books were overflowing.

I knew I was just as skilled as they were, and I worked thirteen times as hard. So why were they having more success?

Deep in my gut, I suspected what the answer probably was. My name. A "black name" like JeVon didn't fit the playbook.

Customers, potential clients, hiring managers; they heard a name they didn't recognize, and consciously or not, they dismissed it.

My gut feeling was confirmed one day when I *did* happen to land a call with a prospective customer. While we were exchanging pleasantries, he asked me, "By the way, what kind of name is JeVon McCormick? You've got a black first name and a white last name!"

So it *was* my name. Well, if they didn't like my name, that was easy enough to change.

The next day, I got new letterhead printed with the name "JT McCormick"—the kind of ethnically ambiguous name I knew would avoid judgment and improve my odds of success.

Just like that, my calls started getting returned and my calendar filled up with appointments.

JeVon McCormick couldn't get a call back. But JT McCormick, obviously of the seasoning empire McCormicks, who probably summered in Maine in between semesters at Yale? Suddenly people were all too happy to open the door for him.

Was it disheartening to have to take this route?

Yes.

Would I do it again?

Yes. I have no regrets. To get in the room back then, I had to play the game. I had to run the old playbook.

I erased all traces of the name JeVon. For almost thirty years, JeVon didn't exist.

Until the year 2020, when it occurred to me that maybe some of the frustration I was feeling was with myself. I was part of the problem.

I had edited myself ruthlessly—to the extent of denying my own name—to make the business world comfortable. And in doing so, I had advanced my career, or really, made a career possible at all.

But now that I was on the other side of the door, sitting atop the mountain I'd climbed, enjoying the fruits of all the unmatched hard work I'd put in, I was still alone.

There were no other JeVons in the boardroom.

How could I expect that to change, when I still wasn't willing to own my own name?

THE PLAYBOOK FILTER

The old playbook that has built American business is there for a reason.

It works. Or, it *worked,* up until recently.

We've never done things any other way, so in effect, there's a confirmation bias happening. The people who are in the board-room because they ran the old playbook look around and see success—and it looks like them. When something has been proven to work, why would you want to change it? Why would you want to bring in a new, untested element that could end up causing disruption?

I truly don't believe that diversity at the top levels of leadership is as homogenous as it is because a black man named Rayvonte was up for the same CEO role as a white man named Tim, and the board considered them both, and went with Tim. I truly don't believe that it's as simple as a conscious choice made to exclude anyone.

For that to be true, Rayvonte would have had to be in the run-ning at all. And he's not. Rayvonte didn't even get close to the room where Tim gained entrance. Rayvonte isn't anywhere on the radar of anyone close to the C-Suite—let alone the hiring managers pulling resumes off the top of the stack.

Rayvonte doesn't even have a resume.

The old playbook is everywhere. It has laid every brick of our business world. We live it. We breathe it. It's upheld in tiny everyday decisions, small moments where people are faced with a choice between something they know well, and something they've never seen before. Which one would you pick? Anyone who says they'd go with the untested unknown is either being dishonest, or has never been in that situation in the first place.

We've never had another model of success. We've never had a leadership culture that *isn't* based on the old playbook.

So, up until now, anyone who wanted to climb to the top *had* to run the old playbook. They had no other play. There was no proof to point to, no Rayvonte in a boardroom to support the case that a person who didn't fit the playbook blueprint might actually benefit a business, rather than what many people fear: that they'll harm it.

It would be foolish of me, and foolish of all of us, to discount the very real fear held by many of today's top leaders.

The fear that change won't just be uncomfortable, it could be disastrous.

The fear that disruption—such a popular buzzword in business writing—is something that only works in the hypothetical, and that in reality, their company culture can't handle a new flavor that rocks the boat.

And most of all, the fear that if they make more room for Rayvonte, there will be less room for *them*.

I'm not going to tell people they shouldn't be afraid. If they have fear, that's theirs to feel and manage. I can't take that fear away, anyway; after all, I'm part of the change that's got them worried.

Because, whether you believe it or not, your enterprise *is* changing. The business world *is* being disrupted. Not just by more

Rayvontes getting into the room, although if I'm any proof, that's starting to happen more and more. The business world is also changing with the accelerated creative destruction brought on by the digital age. Today, the average tenure of a departing S&P 500 CEO is a little over seven years. That's down from a little over ten years as recently as 2015. That churn isn't just with people, either—companies themselves are turning over at a faster rate. In 1965, corporations in the S&P 500 Index had an average tenure on the list of 33 years. In 1990, it was 20 years. By 2026, it'll be 14 years. We're changing faster each year than we did the year before, and the change is happening whether you want it to or not.

The Modern Leader sees this change as an opportunity. They look around at a rapidly changing landscape and think, *what other change can I contribute to this moment?*

The answer is, and always should be, *people*.

Because despite the accelerating change of the business landscape, the rise of diversity and inclusion has not matched pace. It's been almost thirty years since I made the decision to change my name from JeVon to JT. And today, society as a whole remains largely unchanged when it comes to equity in the workplace.

A study by researchers at Northwestern University, Harvard, and the Institute for Social Research in Norway showed that on average, "white applicants receive 36% more callbacks than equally qualified black applicants." This statistic has remained steady over time—no movement toward the positive.

This is not surprising. Black representation at the highest levels of corporate America is abysmal. Black people make up 13.4% of the US population, yet you can literally count on one hand the number of Black CEOs of Fortune 500 companies.

And their names?

Roger Ferguson, Marvin Ellison, and Kenneth Frazier.

The wealthiest Black man in America is named Robert Smith.

That's the old playbook at work. The old playbook leaves out anyone who doesn't look and sound like everyone else who's run the playbook throughout history. It leaves out anyone with an ethnic-sounding name, it leaves out anyone without a pristine academic background, and it leaves out huge pools of talent that could be driving your company into the future and increasing your profits.

You're only seeing a tiny slice of the people who can make a difference in your organization, and it's because you've been conditioned to the playbook filter.

The old playbook has built not just the businesses themselves, but the culture of our business world. It's a shared language, a set of customs—even a way of talking, dressing, and behaving. It's a culture that, if you're on the outside looking in, feels impossible to enter unless you change yourself. Unless you change your story, change your name, change who you are.

That's how the playbook gets reinforced. When the only way to get in the room is to assimilate to the playbook culture, nobody inside the room ever sees anything different. They never question their reality. They never wonder what they're missing, because they don't know there's anything else *to* miss.

And then an event like George Floyd's murder happens. An explosion of anger, grief, and frustration erupts from all sides. Instead of being confined to the culture of the streets, to the place where "those people" live their lives, it spills out into the open. It demands attention. It demands change.

Those inside the room are lost. They're confused. They've had blinders on, and now the world outside those blinders has leaked through—and they're scrambling to keep up, to figure out what to do. They "wish" things would "go back to normal."

That's where you get "action" like pulling Aunt Jemima off the shelves of supermarkets. Great! Problem solved.

That's where you get diversity "initiatives". That's where you get "Chief Diversity Officers." Wash, rinse, repeat. It's not new. And it's not *change*. It's the old playbook dressed up in a diversity costume. It's empathy blackface.

The leaders of the old playbook are looking for someone to tell them what to do. They're looking to check a box. They're not looking to lead. They're looking to follow.

Open your eyes.

The world needs action. Not talk disguised as action.

The company you serve needs leadership. Not lip service, not band-aid initiatives driven by fear and virtue-signaling.

The first action of the Modern Leader is to *open your eyes*. See the playbook filter for what it is. And start to look past it, to the edges of the lens. To the people who have been left out and are waiting on the periphery.

Open your eyes and see everyone you've been missing. They've been there the whole time.

PEOPLE, PROCESS, PROFIT

Why do we say the word *diversity* when what we're really talking about is *people?*

Think about that. What does "diversity" mean? It means more people in the room. It means *all* people in the room. We're talking about people, not some abstract concept.

That's why the concept of the "business case" for diversity has never sat well with me.

You see it all the time: articles, consultant materials, annual keynotes. Pages and pages of writing that details how companies can "justify" an inclusion mindset and practice. Endless opinion pieces that rationalize spending on diversity programs.

This way of thinking reinforces the old playbook. It does so in two ways: first, by carving out a whole section of people that haven't fit the business mold, grouping them under a banner called "diversity", and making that banner a line item on a company's budget. Instead of being people, they've become an "initiative". It defines them as not belonging.

And second, it makes *diversity* into a catch-all phrase that covers up the truth: if your business isn't diverse, you haven't prioritized people. You've prioritized profit.

But isn't that what businesses are supposed to do? I hear you thinking.

Nobody gets into business unless they're after profit. But there's a difference between *pursuing* profit, and *prioritizing* it, especially over people. The old playbook is built on the false dichotomy that people and profit are at odds, and in order to go after profit, you can't put people first.

That never made sense to me. But then again, I don't fit the old playbook. I may have had to run plays from it in order to get in the room, but that doesn't mean it's a language I speak. In fact, a lot of the time throughout my career, I found myself faced with something from the old playbook—something coworkers, leaders, and mentors told me *it's just the way it's done*—and asked one question: "Why?"

Most leaders feel they're supposed to have all the answers. I look to find answers by asking questions. More often than not, when I've looked at the old playbook and asked *why*, no one could come up with a good answer.

People and profit are not opposites. They don't have to diminish each other. People and profit can enhance each other in a clear upward trend line.

Ask yourself: is your company truly built to put people first?

I would bet that most CEOs and executives everywhere from Fortune 500 companies to first-year startups would answer, "Yes, of course it is." They'd point to proof like company culture, health benefits, and perks like flex time and tuition reimbursement.

Those are great benefits to put in place, and I'd never argue otherwise. But does it truly show that a company is people-first?

I look at the foundational elements of a business in a pyramid shape.

The pyramid has three levels. At the bottom of the pyramid, at its broadest point, you have People. This represents not only that people are the most important part of the business structure, but also that people should take up the largest portion of the company's attention and efforts. Without the foundation, without people, the company goes nowhere—so that's where any great company should spend most of its time.

The second level is Process. This is narrower than the People level, but still requires significant effort and attention.

The third and final level—the tip of the pyramid—is Profit.

This pyramid shape is stable. It will build a company that lasts. It does so by creating an environment where people want to do their best work for the long term.

The pyramid is also low risk; companies that have a strong foundation of effort and attention on people are more able to weather disruption when it arises, and more likely to come through the other side of a storm relatively intact.

What I've found in observing other companies and researching business is that outwardly, companies often characterize their structure as this pyramid. They love to believe that they have a strong people foundation.

Then the storm hits, and the truth comes out: the company is built on this pyramid, all right, but it's missing crucial pieces of its base. What should be a strong foundation of people is actually itself a sharp point—and the company is teetering in the balance. It's at high risk of toppling over.

Business is about *people*. When people come last, so do businesses. Businesses that put people last... *won't* last.

This brings me back to the "business case" for diversity. I'm not alone in questioning that concept. The *Harvard Business Review* published an article in 2020 titled, "Getting Serious with Diversity: Enough Already with the Business Case." They wrote:

Advocates who justify diversity initiatives on the basis of financial benefits may be shooting themselves in the foot. Research suggests that when company diversity statements emphasize the economic payoffs, people from underrepresented groups start questioning whether the organization is a place where they really belong, which reduces their interest in joining it. In addition, when diversity initiatives promise financial gains but fail to deliver, people are likely to withdraw their support for them.

In their efforts to check a box, companies running the old playbook are actually being left behind. In their efforts to "do diversity", they're overlooking what diversity really means: *people*.

Fast Company agrees as well. In a 2020 article titled, "Why the 'business case' for diversity isn't working", they write:

> Corporate leaders would be better served if they stopped trying to justify diversity with profit margins and stock charts—a mentality that can ultimately hurt the very groups these policies are meant to help—and instead embrace diversity because it is the right thing to do.

Straight to it: If you need to make a business case for why people come first, you probably shouldn't be in business.

The Modern Leader puts people first, knowing that people, process, and profit go hand in hand. They don't do it *because* they'll make more profit, but they do it knowing that, by leading with a people-first mindset, profit will follow.

Recently, I attended a conference where I caught up with a

fellow CEO I've traveled in the same circles with for years. We traded updates on our companies, our kids, and what we're facing in the business world this year. The subject of "DEI"—an acronym I detest, but more on that later—came up.

"We've been putting a ton of resources into DEI this year," this CEO told me, lighting up like a Christmas tree. He rattled off a laundry list of, as he called it, "stuff they were doing". In the entire conversation, he didn't mention the name of one person. He didn't even say the word "people". Not once.

To him, diversity—or DEI—was a trophy he could show off to signal to the world that his company was paying attention to the times. It had nothing to do with people.

THE FLOOD

I never saw myself as someone who was born with privilege. The idea was ludicrous to me. How do you call a kid who goes to bed hungry most nights privileged?

Recently, though, I came to an important realization brought on by the ongoing discussion—if you can call it that—of race relations in America. All the time, I hear people say, "I can't speak to that." Usually it's a white person referring to the black American experience. And they're right; they can't speak to that.

Well, I can. I realized that I was born with one privilege: as a mixed race person, I can speak to both sides. What's more, I can speak to the unique experience of being mixed race, which is not the same as the black experience, nor is it anything like the white experience.

A year and a half ago, I was interviewed for the cover story of a CEO leadership magazine. I learned I'd be sharing the cover with the likes of retired four-star US general David Petraeus, hedge fund billionaire Leon Cooperman, and Anheuser-Busch US CEO Michel Doukeris, amongst others.

As I humbly took in the moment, the interviewer asked what my name, JT, stood for.

"JeVon Thomas," I told him.

"Oh," he said, "you've got an athlete's name!"

In that moment, I faced a choice many professionals of color face: I could lose my temper on the interviewer and "set him straight" for his ignorant comment, or bite my tongue and still land the cover story. I chose the latter, although it's a choice I shouldn't have been forced to make.

People like that interviewer—who later told me how "articulate" I was—are the reason that, thirty years ago, I changed my name from JeVon to JT.

People like Rayvonte, the kid who has no idea what might be possible for someone like him, are the reason I changed it back.

I can recognize that it's no longer just about me. I have a responsibility to those who come after me.

I want the next generation of would-be leaders to see my name—and maybe see theirs—up on a magazine cover, alongside the names of the old playbook.

I reclaimed my name not for myself, but for every kid who comes from the environment and communities I came from. I did it for every Rayvonte out there. Maybe one day, they can enter corporate America and work next to a JeVon, not just a JT.

Is corporate America ready to open their eyes?

I believe that a large portion of it isn't. The leaders of the old playbook are still coming to terms with the fact that they have to, as so many of them put it, "deal with this". That they have to deal with the future. That they have to deal with *me*.

On a recent podcast, the host asked me, "How would you describe yourself? Your work ethic? Your values and beliefs?"

I said, "If we're going to combine all those, then, I'm like a flood. Have you ever seen a flood? It's going to go over, around, under, and through anything in its path. It's happening. JeVon is happening to you."

I'm the mixed-race son of a black pimp father—who, I learned later, fathered 23 children—and an orphaned white single mother.

I grew up on welfare.

I'm also a multi-millionaire who taught himself the skills to go from broke to wealthy—twice.

I'm a husband and father.

I'm an author and a sought-after speaker.

I'm the President and CEO of a company that was named the #1 Company Culture in America. I've been awarded the Best CEO in Austin.

I'm inside the room now. I'm ready to open the door for everyone else.

I'm a Modern Leader.

And my name is JeVon.

CHAPTER 2

LEADERSHIP LESSONS FROM MY PIMP FATHER

THE FIRST TIME I EVER THOUGHT ABOUT WHAT IT MEANS to put people first was watching my pimp father talk to his prostitutes.

When I was nine years old, my father would take me along on his trips to collect money from the women who worked for him. We'd ride through Dayton in his candy-apple-red 1979 Cadillac Eldorado, stopping at street corners where the prostitutes stood waiting for business. My dad would roll down the window; they'd pass him a stack of cash. We'd move on.

This ritual happened no matter the season, rain or shine. Even in winter. If you've never been to Dayton, Ohio in winter, believe me: it's brutal. It's gray, snowy, windy, and freezing cold. The temperature hovers in the 20s. And prostitutes aren't exactly bundled up out there.

I remember women walking up to my dad's car, pulling thin coats around themselves and trying to shield their faces from the icy wind as they paid up. My dad didn't seem to notice their discomfort, or maybe he didn't care. We were toasty warm inside the Cadillac with the heat blowing. I noticed that sometimes the women would stand chatting with my dad longer than usual. I realized later that they were trying to soak up the warmth through the open window as long as possible.

One day, we pulled up to collect from one lady I saw often. It was just below freezing that day, and all she had on was a thin jacket with fake fur around the collar and wrists.

My dad rolled down the Cadillac window, and she stuck her money through the opening.

"It's cold out here," she said. "Can I come in the car? I made my account."

I remember how ashy her skin looked, how she had goosebumps. She was shivering.

My dad said, "You know, sweetheart, no. Get back out there.

You're on a roll. You're doing good, girl. Keep it going, keep it going. When I come back around the next time you can pick dinner."

The lady nodded, but her face was disappointed. We moved on.

The next woman we pulled up to looked nervous. She didn't have any coat or jacket at all. When she stuck her money through the window, and my dad counted it, it turned out she was quite a bit short.

He lost his temper and unloaded on her, shouting every foul name in the book at her.

She started crying. She was shaking from the cold, her teeth chattering.

"Bitch, get out there and get my money. Don't be common." My dad rolled up the Cadillac window and drove off.

I thought to myself: *I wonder how much more money I could make if I was nice to the prostitutes?*

If I was nicer to them, if I let them come in from the cold, if I didn't yell at them and make them cry, they'd probably all want to come work with me, instead of my dad.

We drove through the gray streets of Dayton in winter, and I was lost in thought, looking out the window at the passing shops and piles of brown, muddy snow next to the curbs.

I could make more money in volume, with just a little spent on treating them better.

Competition would be tight, though. The other pimps would be mad at me because I'd start taking their women.

But that was just a problem to be solved. As my father traversed the city streets collecting from his prostitutes, I followed the rabbit hole in my mind all the way down. I thought about how I could scale the business, how I could ultimately make it worth more than all the other pimps' businesses combined.

I hadn't learned yet that a business based on exploiting women could never be people-first. In my child mind, my dad's business was like any other.

At the age of nine, with no education in business other than watching my dad's illegal dealings, I *knew* that putting people first would mean a stronger business. It would mean more profit; it would mean growth. And it would mean that these women wouldn't have to shiver, crying, outside in the cold. At least not because of me.

The memory of that day has never left me. Today, when I'm in conference rooms and mastermind groups, when I'm hearing other CEOs and business leaders break down complex problems, my mind often goes to my father's pimp business.

It wasn't the same business education you get running the old playbook, but it was still a hell of an education.

The kind of education you *only* get when you come from streets like the ones I grew up in.

Over the years, that education has come in handy. I've asked questions no one else even thought to ask. I've been able to see creative solutions to problems that few others could solve.

I'm not alone in that education.

There is pure genius sitting in low-income communities. And beyond. Do you know how much business acumen is sitting in prison right now?

There's a wealth of talent, knowledge, and innovation waiting to be tapped, but you'd never know it. Why? Because the old playbook has trained us to think genius looks like one thing, and one thing only—and it's not the leadership lessons I learned from my pimp father.

There is gold to be found in streets like mine.

And the old playbook ignores it.

The Modern Leader can see what's beyond the playbook filter. They understand that they're missing out on greatness just beyond their field of vision.

A TALE OF TWO DRUG DEALERS

Let me tell you a story about a drug dealer I once knew.

Well, I didn't just *know* her; I *dated* her.

That's right. My ex-girlfriend, the drug dealer. Something I admired about her was how well she understood the number one rule of dealing drugs: if you get people hooked, you'll never run out of customers.

Every drug dealer knows the rule that the first sample is free. Why? Because they want you to get a taste. You'll be back for more, and you'll keep coming back. My ex-girlfriend made this the cornerstone of her sales strategy. Every day, she went around to street level distributors and gave them samples to hand out to potential customers. The samples worked just like they were meant to: they got people hooked. Soon, she had a pipeline of addicted users. Business was good, and she was good at the business.

She was rewarded by the higher-ups she worked for. Soon, she had a company car to drive, a cellphone just for business, a laptop, and an expense account. She had a six-figure income with annual bonuses.

The only real difference between my ex-girlfriend and the kids I saw slinging drugs in the back alleys of Dayton?

What *they* were doing was illegal. Some of them are in prison today because of their activities. Meanwhile, my ex-girlfriend was able to buy herself a half-million-dollar house with the money she made.

I remember when we were first dating and I asked her what she did for a living. "I'm a pharmaceutical rep," she said.

Like so many things I came across in my journey out of the streets, I had no clue what that meant, and I had to ask what a pharmaceutical rep was. When she explained it to me, I was blown away.

"So... you go around to the doctors' offices where people are getting their drugs, and you give them new ones to sell to customers, to get them hooked?"

She looked a little put off. (Not so put off that we didn't date another three months, though.)

"I wouldn't put it that way," she said. "That makes me sound like a... like a *drug dealer* or something."

The way she said the words *drug dealer* told me that she was talking less about the role, and more about the type of person she imagined occupied that role. And yet any of the kids I knew back in Dayton probably would have *crushed* her when it came to sales volume and repeat customers. Their hustle couldn't be matched.

I am blown away that corporate America hasn't yet figured this out: some of the greatest business talent is working two jobs out on the streets, or even serving out a prison sentence.

How much insight, innovation, and knowledge do we have locked up behind bars for selling the same stuff that earned my ex-girlfriend a car and an expense account?

Business is business. At the end of the day, you're selling a product to a customer for a profit. Take it from me: you don't need to attend an Ivy League business school to master the concept. You don't even have to attend high school. Hell, I got my GED handed to me by the janitor, and I've been the President of two companies that have employed hundreds of people and made hundreds of millions in bottom line profit. Business is business.

If I wanted to start a pharmaceutical company, I know exactly where I'd go to build out the sales team. I'd look for and recruit kids who have been nickel-and-dime street corner hustlers and dope slingers. I'd offer those kids full-ride college scholarships and then make them pharmaceutical reps.

Imagine if you said to one of those kids, "Okay, you have to stop thinking small. I'm going to send you to college and then you're going to come work for Pfizer. Your job will be simple: you hand out free samples all day, and you talk to the dealers on the ground—doctor's offices—about why they should be pushing your drugs. We're going to give you a company car, a cell phone, a laptop, and a spending allowance. You'll take doctors and hospital admins out to high-class dinners all the time. If you do really well this year, you'll get a bonus."

You'd already have most of them eating out of your hand, but then you'd drop the mic with the next sentence.

"And you'll never go to jail."

I don't like the term "recruit and retain" when it comes to people, for reasons I'll talk about in a later chapter. But let's just say, I would have *no* problem with recruitment and retainment if I could give kids from the streets that pitch. It would be the best thing they'd ever heard of.

In every neighborhood, in every city in America, there are kids who have done more business management, growth, performance analytics, and customer service than a recent Wharton grad. Do you have any idea how complex and high-stakes a drug operation is? The number of variables you've got to learn and manipulate in order to get to the top, *without* getting arrested or killed… it takes a fast and creative thinker, follow-through, hustle, attention to detail, and determination to make a business like that work.

Just imagine what all these kids know. Imagine every nugget of wisdom and hard-won experience they could bring to your organization, the kind of insight you'd never find in the old playbook.

RIP UP THE PLAYBOOK

Am I suggesting that your next job fair should be held on inner-city streets and cater to drug dealers?

No. That wouldn't work for your business, and it likely wouldn't work for anyone you managed to hire out of such an event. The barriers between worlds right now are too high.

That's why you often hear opponents of any kind of diversity hiring bring up an idea like that as an absurd argument against the concept. "What, so I'm just supposed to go hire *drug dealers* and *convicts* now?" It's a silly straw man argument, but I hear it all the time. Also, if you immediately equate "diversity" with "drug dealers and convicts"—or for that matter, any one race or gender—in your mind, you may want to step back and examine that first.

Bringing down those barriers between worlds, or at least making them a little shorter so that each side can peek over the top at the other—*that's* what I'm talking about.

You're not going to fix racial equity in the workplace with a single hire. It was a long road getting to where we are, and it's going to be a long road out.

A Modern Leader understands that small steps now reap big rewards for the future. And that just because they can't do *everything* right now doesn't mean they should do nothing.

Large-scale diversity initiatives lack the kind of future-focused thinking I'm talking about. They're focused on a near-term destination. They're checking off a box. So you get things like hiring quotas. Anyone with a racial background that isn't white, anyone who isn't a man, anyone who isn't straight… pick the minority group, they'll be included in the quota. Hiring managers go after filling that quota and call it a day.

The problem, though, is that all those candidates who made it to the hiring manager's desk in the first place ran the old playbook to get there, regardless of their minority status.

Is that a bad thing? No. I did it. And more minority hires in the workplace is a step in the right direction.

But it doesn't knock down the barriers between worlds. It doesn't reach out to the JeVons stuck on the streets who couldn't run the playbook even if they wanted to.

Instead of focusing just on increasing minority numbers *right now*, what if we also focused on building for the future by ripping up the playbook?

The next time on-site interviews are scheduled at your company, go out to where the candidates are waiting and take a look around. You'll likely see mostly white faces, a good mix of men and women, perhaps a couple people of color. You might look at the group and think, *Good, we're doing the thing. We're doing diversity.*

I guarantee you that most, if not all, of the candidates sitting there waiting to be interviewed had to run the old playbook to get in the room.

And, should they get the job, they'll have to keep running that playbook just to keep it.

They'll have to do what I did. Edit themselves. Blend in. Assimilate. Leave behind their stories, their culture, their names.

I pride the company I lead, Scribe Media, on the diversity of our tribe. We have a wealth of backgrounds, histories, and stories that contribute to our culture, and it shows in our success. We also have worked hard to build a culture and a company that truly puts people first. This is proven in testimonial after testimonial on our website, anonymous reviews on job sites, and it's written in our Culture Bible as our very first value: We Do Right by People.

Even with all the evidence in the world that we have an inclusive culture where you can bring your whole self to work, the ghost of the old playbook exists. We have one tribe member, a black woman, who in her interviews for the role asked specifically about our Culture Value of Bring Your Whole Self to Work. She asked, "I know Scribe doesn't have a dress code. But am I going to be allowed to wear a head wrap to the office if I want to?"

Our answer was an enthusiastic "Yes, of course." But the reason she was asking is that, at so many other companies, the answer would be, "No, that's unprofessional." That's been her experience.

Corporate America has always been predominantly white, so the culture of the old playbook is white culture. To run the old playbook, it's not just about getting in the room. You have to learn a whole language and set of customs you may not know. If there's a reference to something you've never heard of, you're left out of the conversation.

How many times has someone in your workplace dropped a reference to a TV show or movie "everyone saw as a kid" to make a point, and most people in the room laughed and nodded in understanding?

Well, guess what. We don't all grow up watching the same shows. In fact, up until recently, Hollywood segregated their content into audiences determined by race. You have your white movies and your black movies. You have an entire TV network just for black TV shows: BET.

The next time a reference is made that you assume everyone understands—because "it's something *everyone* knows, right?"— take a look around the room. Ask yourself: is everyone in on the joke?

Is everyone being included?

Are there people in the room who have just been reminded, for the millionth time, that they don't fit the old playbook?

Fitting in is often talked about as a nice-to-have, but in many ways, it's crucial to success. People are naturally motivated to work with people who they understand, and who understand them in return. It's easier. They have the same language and context. There's less miscommunication. There's a shared history to draw from.

If someone doesn't fit the playbook because they're from a culture far outside the playbook, in subtle ways, they're not going to get the same energy put into teaching, coaching, and mentoring them. They're not going to be thought of first when opportunities come around. You're going to pick someone who's more of a sure bet. Someone you relate to. I believe most of the time this isn't even a conscious choice. It's human nature to gravitate toward what you know.

I'll never forget a man I knew early on in my career, Cecil. Cecil was the first black man I ever saw in a business suit. I'd see black men wearing suits in church, or pimps on the streets wearing colorful suits, but never on the job. Cecil became my role model for how to present myself in the business world. Every time I saw him, he was sharply dressed in a three-piece suit, his entire look was impeccable, and if you asked him how he was doing, he'd say, "Tremendous! I'm tremendous."

Every day, Cecil *had* to be tremendous. That was his business strategy. Cecil knew that as a black face amongst the faces of the old playbook in his company, he was being watched at every moment. No matter what was going on in his life, he had to be tremendous.

Cecil never got to show his coworkers deep down who he was. He never got to experience the full support of the people he worked with.

To this day, whenever anyone asks me how I'm doing, I say, "I'm excellent." Cecil's example has stayed with me all this time.

A VIEW OF WHAT'S POSSIBLE

When I mentor young kids from lower-income communities here in Austin, I like to get a sense of their view of life's possibilities.

Often I'll say to a crowd of kids, "Okay, guys, what does *rich* look like? Tell me who's rich."

What do I hear in response?

Lil Wayne. Drake. LeBron.

Don't get me wrong, those men have done well for themselves. But then I ask the kids, "How many of you have heard of Michael Dell?"

Total silence.

I've never met a kid from a low-income community who knows who Michael Dell is. They see Drake as rich—and compared to them, or the average American, Drake is rich. Michael Dell, on the other hand, isn't worth millions or a hundred million. He's worth over $55 *billion*. Drake doesn't have a fraction of his money.

Kids from the streets don't even know what's possible for them. They see the pinnacle of success as being a rapper or athlete. I wrote in *I Got There* that the only choices ever presented to me when I was young were rapper, athlete, and drug dealer. No one ever showed me business. Or, no one ever showed me *legitimate* business—my father's pimp business showed me something, but it wasn't the height of possibilities. The only businesses where I lived were payday loans, pawn shops, and liquor stores.

Modern Leadership isn't about saving every last kid from the streets. It's not about pulling drug dealers off the streets and installing them in boardrooms. Modern Leadership is about realizing your responsibility simply to teach and show what's possible. Opening your eyes goes both ways; there's a world of eye-opening that can be done for kids who have no idea what options they have for their future. They can't picture a life and career like the one I have now. I know I couldn't.

My eyes were opened by my father, not just in the way he ran his business, and the way I would have done it differently. My father literally showed me what was possible past the seedy apartments, crack houses, hourly motels, and outright homelessness that created the landscape of my childhood. When we lived in Houston, my father once took me driving out to a neighborhood called River Oaks, one of the most expensive neighborhoods in the country. It ranks right up there with Beverly Hills.

I had never seen anything like it—I had never *imagined* anything like it. It was like driving through a different world. The homes in River Oaks weren't just mansions, they were palaces. The bright green lawns were perfectly manicured and extended what seemed like the length of a city park as they wrapped up and around the multi-story, sprawling estates. The driveways weren't just strips of asphalt to park your car on; they were roads unto themselves. Many of the homes had columns on the front porch like something out of a history book.

Driving though that neighborhood shattered my view of what was possible for my life. *If this exists*, I thought, *I want it.*

All my father did was open my eyes. It wasn't even his intention to do so; he could have been driving through that neighborhood for any number of reasons, but inspiring me wasn't one of them. Showing me what existed wasn't the same as showing me how to get it, and he certainly didn't help me get there. But before he opened my eyes, my ideas of the future were confined to a narrow lane. With my eyes open, my world was expanded. I started wondering just how much might be out there for me. All I had been thinking about was getting off the streets. Now I was thinking about getting *in* one—the kind of neighborhood where people weren't just rich, but wealthy. Just knowing that was possible changed the direction of my dreams.

Recently, I was invited to speak at a conference where the majority of the attendees were in corporate finance. Often, at these kinds of events, my keynote stands out from the rest starkly. Nothing against the wisdom being shared by other speakers, but getting up on stage in front of an old playbook audience and dropping business lessons from my black pimp father tends to shake things up in a way no one sees coming.

The conference organizer and I prepped for my appearance beforehand. We got to talking about how Scribe Media has built its culture on putting people first.

The organizer said that empathy was a hot topic at the moment. "Tell me about empathy," she said. "With a childhood like yours, how did empathy show up? What examples did you see?"

In my mind, I thought immediately of the shivering prostitute being told she couldn't come into the car and warm up.

How did empathy arise in that context?

I was very direct with her. I told her that, when I was nine, I went out with my dad collecting money from prostitutes. I saw the way he treated them, and how no matter how cold it was, he made them stand outside and work for him. So, in that world, empathy was something that came from me wondering if there was another way to run that business. Empathy was me asking myself, could my dad treat those women better, and what would happen if he did?

The biggest lesson I learned from my pimp father was this:

You can't put a price on empathy.

I hear often from CEOs and business leaders, "We're trying to build diversity in hiring. We've got the door wide open. But qualified applicants are just not applying. They're not coming to us."

I ask, is the door truly wide open, if more diverse candidates can't even see their way to it? If no one has helped open their eyes to what's possible?

Or if they do make it all the way to the door, walking through it means leaving behind the most personal parts of themselves in order to fit the old playbook?

Modern Leadership isn't a new playbook. The Modern Leader is ready to throw away the entire playbook, rip it up, and lead without an instruction manual. Modern Leadership isn't passive. It's active.

Leadership is an *action*. And Modern Leaders lead from the front.

CHAPTER 3

❧

MADE IN AMERICA

"WHAT ARE YOU?"

I've been asked that question more times than I can count.

Growing up half black, half white in Dayton, there weren't a
lot of other kids who looked like me. Anyone who's mixed race
knows that the features you end up with are a tossup. Skin color,
hair color and texture, eye color—there's a lot in your DNA to
choose from. I've never looked white, but I've also never looked
"stereotypically black". When I was a kid, people didn't know
what to make of me.

The world was a lot different back then. Today, I see mixed-race
people being celebrated for their unique "look". Back in the

1970s, there was no celebration. Instead, I got people asking me "what" I was.

The first time I heard that question, I was barely old enough to make the memory.

But I did make that memory, and I remember it to this day.

I remember how badly those words stung. I remember how confused I was. *What do you mean, what am I?* I thought. *I'm human. I'm JeVon.* I couldn't understand what they were asking. I knew they weren't asking out of curiosity or kindness, though. I knew there was something dark behind the words.

Even as a little kid, I understood that being asked that question meant I was different. Why would anyone ask what I was, unless I was obviously not what *they* were?

I get that question much more rarely now—last I heard it was a couple of months ago. Society has come a long way. But I'm also sure that the world I've built for myself, as an author and business leader, does its part to shield me from a certain level of disrespect. I'm sure that question is thrown in the face of thousands of people each day. People who don't have the title, the money, or the status that I've worked hard to attain. People whose appearance, way of being, way of identifying, or way of loving doesn't match up with the status quo.

And nowhere is the status quo still more prevalent than in the American workplace.

Yes, many companies have done away with dress codes, and have relaxed some of the more formal rituals that used to characterize the way we all showed up to the office each day. On the surface, the status quo is a little less rigid.

But the way we dress and talk is just the tip of the iceberg. The old playbook's threads are so deeply woven into every room, wall, and carpet in every office building that it can be difficult to see and recognize how it's still holding people back.

If you walk into a room and stick out, you might roll with that for a while. You might try to make it work.

Eventually, though, it's exhausting to be different. It takes too much energy to constantly be the one everyone's trying to figure out. Being a "what" instead of a "who".

Even the way companies often go about diversity initiatives contributes to the unspoken otherness placed on minorities. A report titled "Being Black in Corporate America," by the Center for Talent Innovation, found that even though many companies have implemented diversity and inclusion programs, those programs often do nothing more than erase black experiences by creating a culture that dictates how to contribute only in ways that white people are comfortable with. So, by "inclusion", these programs often actually mean "assimilation".

Many companies will institute a "celebration" day or week, holding up some aspect of a culture—whether it be a nationality, a sexual orientation, or even a sex or gender itself—under a spotlight. Everyone takes time out of their workday to acknowledge the otherness of that group, and it's called celebration.

I'm not saying *no one* appreciates gestures like that, because I don't speak for everyone. But I don't appreciate it. I'm already contorting myself to just be seen for my work and who I am—don't pull me out and shine a spotlight on me all day as a "what" instead of a "who".

My experience in the past thirty years was one of erasure. I erased my name, until I reclaimed it in 2020. I erased my past, until I wrote and shared my story in *I Got There*. And I erased what made me unique, until I helped build a company culture that allowed my individuality to exist in its fullest expression.

Ask yourself: Why do individuals feel the need to edit themselves to fit into our organizations?

Why don't we instead edit our organizations to better fit individuals?

As a Modern Leader, your first action is to open your eyes. But what if you do that, take a look around at your company, and all you see is yourself?

Opening your eyes is meaningless if all you're willing to see is what you've always seen. A Modern Leader works to build a culture that acknowledges, respects, and values the individual histories and experiences of each team member, rather than asking people to erase what makes them unique for the sake of everyone else's comfort.

INSIDE, BUT STILL OUTSIDE

When I changed my name to JT, I did it so that I could get into "the room".

But once I was inside, I found myself still on the outside in almost every other way.

I believe the whole reason I got hired at the insurance company I worked at when I was eighteen, my first office job, is because my mom worked there. Someone named JeVon with a GED never would have gotten in the door otherwise.

Once I was in, I immediately realized that nobody was going to help me assimilate. Fifty percent of my time the first few months at that job was just trying to catch up on the ways of the old playbook.

In some ways, corporate America is very similar to the streets. You don't go into certain "hoods" wearing certain colors and logos; in corporate America, there are also unspoken rules about colors, outfits, even which shoes you can wear. When I first started at the insurance company, I had no clue about any of the rules. The environment was so far out of my experience that my next-door neighbor had to teach me how to tie a tie.

No one teaches you the unspoken rules of corporate America. That's especially true if you come from a neighborhood like mine. Sometimes I felt like I was hearing a foreign language, even though everyone was speaking English. The language of business wasn't one I had any fluency in, and it seemed like most other people somehow knew it like the back of their hand.

Learning this language meant opening myself up to embarrassment. I had to ask questions constantly to figure out what was going on, what people were talking about. I've built a career on asking questions, and I'm always willing to risk looking foolish in order to learn what I need to know. Sure, I might get strange looks, but at least I come away knowing something that will get me another step toward the future my father showed me driving through River Oaks.

I remember early on in my career I heard the phrase "401k" so many times at the office that I thought it must be a room number.

So, one day I asked the question: "Where's conference room 401k?"

My question was met with confusion, then laughter.

Moments like that happen every day for anyone who didn't come up running the old playbook. When you don't speak the unspoken language of business, you constantly risk being exposed. Exposed to ridicule, to being laughed at, to someone figuring out you "don't belong". And you begin to fear that if everyone figures out you don't belong, maybe they'll start questioning if you should even be there in the first place.

That's not an irrational fear—it's real. It happens. People *do* question it, not directly, but in code.

The unspoken language of corporate America? That language has a code name: *professionalism*.

Having to explain things to people who don't speak the language of professionalism? That's where you hear code terms like *language barrier* or *culture barrier*.

What I believe people really mean with that code is simply that they're uncomfortable. They're having to make space for the unfamiliar, and it's not as easy as it once was to understand everyone they work with. It takes effort. Effort they're not used to having to expend.

In my experience, the willingness to expend that effort gets higher when someone is white versus a minority race. Even if we come from the same depths of poverty, a JeVon is going to have fewer opportunities than a Steve. Steve is far more likely to be taken under someone's wing and taught the ways of corporate America. JeVon is going to have to figure it out on his own.

My experience is not unique. I worked hard to get in the room, but once inside, I realized I was still on the outside. I got there, but once I did, I realized that I was still miles off target.

ASK QUESTIONS

People who rise to the level of CEO more often than not come from a privileged background. Fact.

And there's nothing wrong with that.

My four children are leading a very privileged life; they live in a gated community, they attend private Christian school, and they've never known food or shelter insecurity. They have two happily married parents who show them attention and love. They can't help that.

Just like I can't help that I was born into the slums of Dayton, another CEO can't help that they were born into security. I often see privilege being held against the privileged as though they did something *wrong* in having more money, security, and opportunities than other people. I've never understood that. You play the hand you're dealt in life, because what else are you going to do?

As a CEO, coming from privilege definitely gave you a leg up in running the old playbook. A Modern Leader acknowledges that. It doesn't mean you didn't work hard, or that you had everything handed to you on a silver platter. But it does mean that you had a head start. You were fluent in the unspoken language of corporate America before you even knew you were speaking it. You had opportunities other kids didn't, and if you're a CEO now, then in all likelihood, you leveraged those opportunities into accomplishments and success.

In other words, you did exactly what a person *should* do when given an advantage, in my opinion: you made the most of it.

But coming from privilege, running the old playbook from Day 1, being fluent in the language of corporate America—these also represent a significant challenge.

Because you've never seen through any other lens besides the old playbook, it's the only language you know. And that means that when it comes to connecting with the people you serve, you might only know how to connect with and relate to people like you.

A leader's role is to serve *everyone* in the company they lead, and service means connection. Ask yourself: how do you plan to lead a future-focused company culture, a culture that attracts, welcomes, celebrates, and appreciates people from *all* diverse backgrounds, if you can't connect with them once they make it into the room?

This is where Modern Leadership stands in stark contrast to traditional leadership. A Modern Leader knows that it's no one's *fault* how or where they were raised, or how much or how little privilege they were born with. But the Modern Leader knows it's their *responsibility* to serve every single person they lead, regardless of the effort it takes to build a bridge toward a shared language.

A Modern Leader knows that they're responsible for creating an environment of safety. They're responsible for creating a company culture that is *strengthened* by differences, not diminished. They're responsible for putting in the extra effort to make sure every single person feels welcomed, seen for who they are, and safe in expressing themselves.

When I'm at conferences with other CEOs, one of the biggest complaints I hear about employees is accountability, or the lack of it. I hear people complain about how their employees lack motivation, follow-through, and ownership. That when things at their company go wrong, no one wants to be "left holding the bag", so no one "owns up".

That sounds like a culture problem to me. And a culture problem starts with the CEO. Period.

Ask yourself this question: *Why* aren't the people you lead taking accountability?

Then ask yourself a second, harder question: What, as the leader, are you doing—or *not* doing—to create a culture of accountability?

What tone are you setting?

Are the people you lead *safe?*

Accountability arises from safety. When people know they're safe, that they're not going to get kicked out the door for mistakes—or for asking questions like "Where's conference room 401k"—they're more likely to take accountability.

On the other hand, if you're someone from outside the old playbook, and you made it into the room, but you can't connect with anyone once you're inside—you're not going to feel safe. You're going to be waiting to be found out. Exposed.

The old playbook creates a subtle culture of fear for anyone who exists outside its filter.

The funny thing is, I see the same fear among traditional CEOs faced with the changing business landscape. I see the same lack of accountability in them they so often complain about. So many old playbook leaders won't take accountability for their companies' lack of diversity. In this way, they're also affected by the subtle culture of fear that arises from the old playbook. They're also afraid of being exposed. They're afraid of the future. They don't see themselves in it, and they're afraid they're being left behind. They don't know how to connect to the people outside the old playbook, yet they're being pressured by society to let those people in the room. They're afraid of being called out. They're afraid of saying the wrong thing. They're afraid of asking the wrong questions.

So they're asking *no* questions.

I've heard CEOs who struggle with company diversity grumble, "How am I supposed to know everyone's background? How am I supposed to know about their lives?"

It's simple. *Ask questions.* Listen, learn, and seek to understand.

I don't believe there's such a thing as right or wrong questions. I don't believe there are good or bad questions.

Thirty years ago, I'm sure my coworkers thought me asking about the 401k room was a *bad* question, and more specifically, a stupid question.

But it got me one step closer to fluency in the language of corporate America, so I disagree. I don't care how stupid someone else might think I look; I'm never going to *not* ask the question when I don't know something.

Even today, as CEO, I pause meetings to ask what certain words mean, or ask for breakdowns of concepts I haven't learned yet. My role as CEO is to surround myself and the company with people smarter than me. That means I'm sometimes in the dark when the people I serve bring their knowledge to the table. When that happens, why wouldn't I ask questions and learn as much as possible?

I know leaders who are afraid of being exposed for not knowing *everything*. They fear that asking questions will reveal to the people they lead that they shouldn't be the leader. They fear losing the trust of those they serve.

Ask yourself: *are you sure you have their trust in the first place?*

If you're not willing to ask them questions about their lives, to learn about their backgrounds and connect with them as individuals, for fear of saying or asking the wrong thing—then why *should* they trust you?

A Modern Leader's accountability encompasses truly seeking to understand the circumstances of everyone in your organization. It's your role to know where they're coming from, and what's keeping them from where they want to go.

Ask questions.

A trend I've noticed in our society of late is the shaming of certain questions. This is especially true for questions about race, culture, sexuality, gender identity, and background. I've heard people say, "If you have to ask that question, you're not paying attention." I've also heard, "It's not my job to educate you."

I call bullshit on that mindset. The alternative to asking questions is staying ignorant. If we shame people for their curiosity—even if we feel they *should*, for whatever reason, already know the answer—then we're guaranteeing the perpetuation of ignorance. We're keeping everyone in the dark.

The old playbook thrives in the dark. Modern Leadership shines a light on it.

I don't speak for black people, white people, mixed-race people, victims of childhood abuse, or poor kids from Dayton. I only speak for myself. I would *always* prefer to educate someone when they've curiously sought to understand more about me. I would always prefer to extend a hand with knowledge, rather than judge or shame someone's lack of knowledge.

A Modern Leader opens their eyes by asking questions.

All questions.

MADE IN ALL OF AMERICA

I hate the word "acceptance".

I hear it all the time in conversations about diversity and inclusion. People talk about needing to promote acceptance like it's a far-reaching goal.

Acceptance isn't the finish line—it's barely across the starting line. The word acceptance implies judgment, because it implies the premise that there's a possibility people like me might *not* be accepted.

Obviously, I know that's not just a possibility, that's a reality for many people around the world. But it seems to me that we can do far better than *acceptance*, which is the final stage of grief.

Acceptance isn't the lowest bar possible—in my opinion, that's *tolerance*, another word that implies a dark alternative—but it's only one step above it.

People don't want corporate America's acceptance. People don't want their tolerance.

People want to be *welcomed.*

Why is that so much to ask for? Why is it even a question in our society that some people might not be welcomed in the workplace, exactly as they are, without having to edit themselves to fit a playbook?

When I was first starting out in business, there was *no* part of my background that would have been welcomed in the workplace. I'd hear other people bring up stories about their parents, their brothers and sisters, their cousins. I'd hear them tell stories from their childhood that helped them connect with their coworkers and showed a little bit of who they were.

I can only imagine the reaction if I'd joined in with an anecdote about my black pimp father or my 23 siblings. Or, leaving that aside—stories about life on the streets wouldn't have been welcomed, either.

And yet that life on the streets prepared me for the business world in its own unique way. No, it wasn't an Ivy League MBA. Even so, every day as a CEO I come across situations that stump other colleagues, but that I can see a creative solution to because of something I learned watching illegal dealings in my childhood, or experiencing homelessness—or even just the patchwork quilt of attendance that was my public school education before I got my GED.

When I was fifteen, I took a standardized intelligence test. When the results came back, I was told I wasn't smart. I was "below average" in intelligence. At the age of 15, I was reading at a 5th grade level.

Much later in life, I realized that what I was given wasn't a test of intelligence. It was a test of "what I knew"—but only of the standard school curriculum, which I'd had limited experience with. Did that mean I didn't know anything? *Hell no*. I knew about things most other fifty-year-olds couldn't imagine. Yet according to the state, I was below average intelligence.

Once, as part of another test to place me in a grade at a new school, I was given a book to read. I struggled with it, so they gave me a different book at a lower reading level. Same story. Finally, they handed me a Little Golden Book. That's right—the books your kids probably got started reading when they were six or seven.

I was devastated. No one seemed to care that I was struggling, and no one asked why. All they cared about was telling me how I didn't fit their curriculum. No one cared about trying to make the curriculum fit me.

Decades later, when I became the CEO of a publishing company, I found myself working with Harvard grads, professional writers, designers, and editors. These were people who had written and published hundreds of books between them. They were experts. When it came to books, they knew what they were doing.

I was confused by one of the first things I noticed in the book-writing process. After working with a professional writer to talk out all their ideas and content, an author would wait excitedly to see their finished manuscript. When it came time to deliver it, our company would simply send it over in one big file—thirty to fifty thousand words in a dozen or more chapters, dumped on the author all at once. It was then their responsibility to read the manuscript and prepare to edit it.

This seemed nerve-wracking to me. So, as usual, I asked questions. "Why do we drop the whole book on the author all at once?"

The book experts were unanimous in their responses: "We can't break it apart. We have to deliver it all at once. They need to read it straight through. This is how it's done."

Having worked within this process to write my book with the company—that's right, I came to the company I now serve as CEO as a client myself—I cringed imagining opening my email to a giant book, all my words, thoughts, stories, and voice, that I would need to read in its entirety. It seemed like a recipe for disaster. If I read the first few pages and didn't like it, or didn't think it sounded like me, there was no way I could bring myself to read a hundred more.

I kept asking questions. "What if they don't like it?"

That's what the revisions process is for.

"Wouldn't it be better to show them a small part of it upfront so they can check the tone and voice before the whole book gets written?"

No, we couldn't do that. You can't write a book that way.

I don't often "drop the three letters", as I call it. I reserve pulling the CEO card for times when I believe so strongly in a decision or direction that I'm willing to go against the collective opinion of our tribe.

In this instance, I knew beyond a doubt that we were making things difficult for many people by dumping a whole book on them all at once. My perspective as a 100% outsider to the world of publishing was a fresh look at a process that hadn't changed in decades.

I kept thinking back to the humiliating reading tests, to being handed the Little Golden Book. How many of our clients might also feel that kind of dread about reading their manuscript if, right off the bat, they weren't feeling the tone?

I asked our team to put together a process that would allow our authors to read a small part of their book before the rest was written, upfront, to hone and approve the tone and voice. It was immediately successful. Authors felt more comfortable reading their entire manuscripts after seeing and approving the tone early on. We avoided tons of wasted time and work by simply course-checking at the start, rather than once we were at the finish line.

All it took was asking questions. Asking *why*. Using the knowledge and wisdom from my non-playbook life and applying it to a situation the playbook-runners were certain they had figured out.

This kind of insight is usually hidden behind the old playbook filter. People who make it into your organization and are immediately swept up in the tide of assimilation might not feel like their unique insights are encouraged. They might not feel like their unique backgrounds and perspectives are welcomed or wanted.

As a Modern Leader, it's your role to welcome them. It's your responsibility to discover the insights you've been missing.

How do you do that?

Ask questions.

Imagine that you've hired someone from outside the old playbook. They interviewed well and display talent and drive, but when they start working in their role, you find out that they're missing some of the basics. Two immediate actions a Modern Leader takes:

One, ask questions to figure out how to assist them. Ask: "What would you like to learn? How can I coach you? How do you prefer to learn and be mentored?" (Notice that I didn't use the word *train*. That's another word I've deleted from my vocabulary, and we'll talk about why in a later chapter.)

Two, ask questions to learn from them what they know that you don't. Ask them about their background, where they came from, and how they see your organization. Ask them what the view looks like from the outside. Not only will you connect with each person you take the time to be curious with, but you'll likely discover holes in your game. You'll find ways you can make your organization even stronger—things you would never see through the old playbook filter.

It boils down to two questions a Modern Leader asks everyone they meet:

What would you like to know, and how can I assist in teaching you?

What do you know that I don't, and how can I learn it from you?

Modern Leadership is a state of constant education. A Modern Leader not only welcomes but seeks to discover and understand every voice, every background, every insight. Listen. Learn. Seek to understand.

From *all* people.

Businesses love to tout as a selling point that they're "made in America". But what this usually means is that they're made in the narrow slice of America that fits the old playbook.

You're not made in America unless you're made in *all* of America.

THE POWER OF HELLO

What am I?

I'm a CEO who got his GED from a janitor.

I'm a child of poverty who worked his way to multi-million-dollar wealth.

I'm a mixed-race person who has a unique viewpoint on the American experience.

I told a story in *I Got There* about a painful but important lesson I once learned from my father, when I failed to say hello to a girl I knew in a store one time. He told me that no matter where someone was from, no matter who they were, they always deserved respect and a hello.

It's another odd lesson from a pimp: that all people deserve politeness and respect. I won't claim this is a philosophy I saw my father live through his actions one hundred percent of the time, but he did teach me the power of hello.

As the leader of an organization, never underestimate the power of what a "hello" can do to change the trajectory of someone's day. I always say that my goal isn't to win the argument, but to move the crowd. There's no better way to move the crowd than to individually connect through a simple hello. A Modern Leader doesn't just see people; they ensure that people know they are *seen*.

When people feel seen, they feel respected. They feel *welcomed.*

That's the culture of the future the Modern Leader will build.

Not acceptance.

Not tolerance.

Welcoming.

I don't care who you love, what pronouns you use, what racial background you have, who you voted for, how you grew up, or where you're from.

I only care about one thing.

Are you happy?

If the answer is *yes*, then you've already won.

And the culture of Modern Leadership has a place for you.

Welcome.

Part Two

OPEN YOUR DOORS

CHAPTER 4

HOW I GOT THERE

YOU MIGHT THINK THE MOST DANGEROUS, CUTTHROAT, watch-your-back environment a minority could ever find themselves in would be the streets.

For me, it wasn't. Corporate America was.

At the insurance company where I started my career, if you were a minority, you had to work at least twice as hard to be recognized. This was never a problem for me, because as I've written before, my personal mantra was: *No one will ever outwork me.*

Should I have *had* to put in 80 hours for every 40 put in by Steve, Tim, and Blake? No, but I did anyway. I knew that was the only way I was getting to my River Oaks future.

I could also tell that, as a minority, I was being watched. It's the same reason why Cecil was never anything less than "tremendous." The rules of the old playbook seemed to apply ten times more strictly to anyone who didn't quite fit its pages. You had to be ultra-professional, ultra-polite, ultra-productive. You had to ultra-assimilate.

God forbid two minorities were seen eating lunch together or hanging out—that would be your identity from that point on. You were "the black group". Didn't matter what you did to fit into the old playbook, or how you edited yourself. You were banding together, and that made people uncomfortable. That made people nervous.

As a result, where I worked, minorities ignored each other. There was no reaching out a helping hand to bring up a fellow person of color. The sense I got immediately was that there was only room for *one* person who looked like me.

While I was working in the mailroom at the insurance company, they hired a Hispanic lady named Maria to work with me. On her first day, I went up to her and said, "Hi, how are you? Great to meet you."

While shaking her hand, I was thinking, *my work ethic is going to destroy you. If the day ever comes when they let one of us go, it's sure as hell not going to be me.*

Working in the mailroom wasn't hard, but you had to be fast and detail oriented. You had to have a sorting system that kept up with the dozens of bins that were stacked inside the door each day. If you fell behind, people upstairs noticed right away. They didn't get important documents they were waiting for; they couldn't do their own jobs. Falling behind wasn't an option.

Maria did her best, but a week into the job, it was clear that she was struggling. She couldn't keep up. I could tell she was watching how fast I whipped through the bins, her eyes nervous as she tried to keep pace.

One day she pulled me to the side. "JT," she asked quietly, "could you slow down a little?"

I asked what she meant. "You're so fast. You're doing two bins for every one I can get through."

I knew that, of course. And I knew why she wanted me to slow down. She was standing out, and not in a good way. As a minority there was no room for her to stand out. She would not be given the benefit of the doubt.

"I have a daughter. I need this job," she said. I knew she was a single mom. For a moment, I saw my own mom in her.

I told her I'd do my best to slow down a little.

And then—I say this with remorse now—I worked even faster.

There could be only one person at that company who didn't fit the playbook, and it was going to be me. I had made it into the room. I wasn't getting kicked out.

It's hard to describe the mix of emotions I felt in that situation. I was frustrated and sad, because Maria deserved a shot just like anyone else. It wasn't fair that the playbook we were trying to run only had one play for people like us. I felt guilty knowing that Maria might not be able to take care of her daughter because of how she compared to me.

But I also felt driven. No one had handed me the playbook, but I'd been able to figure out a play I could run that would get me another ten yards away from the streets. I felt like a running back with the ball under my arm and a clear field out in front of me. Nothing was going to get in my way. And no one was going to catch me.

For minorities, a corporate career often feels like a zero sum game. If there's room for someone else from outside the playbook, that means there's less room for you.

Looking back, it's easy to make the connection in my mind between that zero-sum fear I had as a minority in the workplace, and the fear I see in old playbook leaders now. It's the same concept. More room for others means less room for them. No wonder they're so afraid of that future; it's the present they've watched minorities live for the past sixty years.

I once heard someone say about men who are homophobic:

"They're afraid of men hitting on them because they don't want to be treated the way they've always treated women."

That's what I think of when I see traditional leaders fearful of the future. They're afraid they're going to be treated the way the playbook has always treated anyone who doesn't fit into it.

To make it to my River Oaks future, I had to be cutthroat. I had to turn a cold shoulder to others who were looking for a way in. I had made it into the room, and the only way I'd stay there was by slamming the door shut behind me.

The doors to corporate America aren't just closed by the old playbook leaders who fear losing their own place inside. The doors are also held shut by people like me who make it in and are desperate to stay.

The old playbook makes gatekeepers of us all.

The Modern Leader knows that playbook is played out. They know that space in the room isn't a limited resource. They know there's room for everyone who wants to come inside, and that more people in the room means more rewards for everyone, now and in the future.

Modern Leadership begins with opening your eyes to see everyone outside the playbook that you've been missing.

It continues with opening your doors and inviting them in.

BETWEEN TWO WORLDS

What was my journey to Modern Leadership?

I talked earlier about the unique perspective I have on race relations in America. As a mixed-race person, I've seen both sides of the racial divide.

This didn't always feel like a privilege; in fact, for most of my life, it felt like a burden.

Growing up in the 70s and 80s as the child of a white mother and a black father, I didn't get the benefit of a tribe to belong to. And on the streets, a tribe is everything. A shared identity and group of people you belong with keeps you safe. It keeps you protected. A lot of the time, it might even keep you fed and sheltered.

As a mixed-race kid, I was isolated from any identity or tribe. My black relatives looked at me with resentment and mistrust; to them, I had it *easier* with my lighter skin tone and "good hair". To black people, I was "white boy". I have to laugh thinking back on that idea. White people certainly didn't care that my skin was a few shades lighter than my dad's, my sisters and brothers', my cousins'. To white people, I was definitely *not* one of them. No white person has ever called me "white boy".

To white people, I was just black. To a particular type of white person, a less kind type, I was worse than black. I was the product of a mixed-race union, an abomination that had been illegal less than a decade before. As a child, I heard my mom get called a "nigger lover" more times than I can count, people hatefully spitting the words at her on the street, in grocery stores, at bus stops. We were once evicted from our apartment by one of those less-kind white people, all our belongings thrown out on the curb like trash. So, no, my lighter skin didn't make things easier for me.

I noticed something odd as I got older, though: each side treated me as though I *did* fully belong to the other. This has been especially true of white people, who, through the years, have often asked me for "the black perspective" on certain topics. Or they've asked me questions about the black experience. I said before that I don't believe in good and bad questions—but I'll be honest, I don't love being asked about the black experience. It feels like another little piece of my story being erased.

If you thought we left the one drop rule back in the dark ages where it belongs, try being mixed race in America. It often feels to me like white Americans can only see two races: white, and not white.

You saw this when Obama was elected. Everywhere you went, you heard it: *the first black President.*

That bothered me at the time, and it still bothers me. Obama is mixed race. Like me.

Why is that experience so often erased? Why didn't we celebrate "the first mixed race President"?

Why is that any less progress than electing a black President? Having a white mother, in my experience, didn't reduce the racism I faced. Why would Obama having a white mother diminish being born outside the old playbook and making it to the White House?

The perspective I have is a bridge between two worlds. I wasn't accepted by either side, so I've lived my life in the space between, always peering in from the outside. I had to figure out how to succeed without a tribe. It was lonely, often frightening, and built in me a powerful drive to create a tribe I could be a part of. Because if I wasn't welcomed in either world, then I would need to build a new one where I *was* welcomed.

The seeds of Modern Leadership were planted in my mind from a young age. Every time I didn't belong somewhere, I vowed to create a space where I would. Every time a door was closed to me—or I had to hold a door closed to stay on the other side of it—I dreamed of opening every door I could find. Every time I had to leave a piece of my story behind, I added to the new story I was writing in my head: that one day, I would build a business where every story was welcomed.

THE GET THERE MINDSET

"What would you say to other people from the streets who want to *get there*, but weren't born with your talents?"

I was asked this question at my very first book reading, an event held at Book People in my hometown of Austin, Texas. That night was my entrance into the tribe of published authors. I was nervous, because I didn't pull punches in *I Got There*, and I had never told my story to the world without editing the parts that made people uncomfortable. I was elated to see my own book and my name on the shelf next to big-name authors. I was grateful for the support of my family, my friends, and my tribe, who gave me a huge round of applause and cheers from the audience as I stood at the podium with my book in my hand.

And then, with that question, I was annoyed.

I tried not to snap at the man who had asked the question, but I couldn't keep a little tension out of my tone.

"Let me start by saying: I wasn't born with *anything*," I fired back. "I worked hard for everything I've ever gotten in life."

I've thought about that moment a lot in the five years since that night. Why was I so irritated by that question?

At the time, I took it as an affront. *Born with my talents?* The idea that I'd had it different from any other kid from the streets offended me. It felt like another small erasure, like the sacrifice and struggle I'd endured were being dismissed. Like the reason I "got there" was just because I had talent.

I sure didn't feel talented when the state deemed me "below average intelligence." I didn't feel talented when I was handed a Little Golden Book.

But over the years, the people closest to me have helped me understand something important:

Having talent doesn't erase the hard work.

It's taken me years to admit, but I can acknowledge it now: I do have talent. I have abilities others don't.

The environment I grew up in, if anything, honed those abilities to give me an edge. It took my innate talent for reading people and sharpened it—because where I grew up, reading someone's intentions wrong could be the difference between life and death.

My childhood was the ultimate boot camp for the curiosity and ability to learn fast that I was born with. When you aren't given a playbook, you have to figure it out every step of the way. You have to relentlessly ask questions to avoid making a wrong move, because coming where I came from, a wrong move could be your last move.

Even my talent for business was honed by the way I came up. I didn't learn business sitting in a classroom. I learned it by watching pimps and drug dealers fight for dominance. I learned it by working my way from cleaning toilets to sorting mail to sitting in a boardroom. I learned it by putting in the 80 hours to Steve, Jeff, and Mike's 40. When you aren't given the chance to take it easy, you have to go hard. After a while, you're used to going harder than most other people.

I've said it many times: I'd live my childhood again fifty times over if it gets me to the life I have today. If that was the training ground for everything I've built, I'd do it again.

The biggest influence on how I got there, though, had nothing to do with talent.

I got there because *I chose to.*

I had endured a childhood of abuse, poverty, hunger, fear, homelessness, and loneliness. I had gone to sleep shivering and with an empty belly more nights than any child should (which is zero). I had been cast aside, abandoned, bullied, and laughed at. I had been hurt by people who should have taken care of me.

When I was six and seven years old, I was sexually abused by one of my dad's prostitutes on many different occasions. This was a woman my dad left me and some of his other kids with a lot of the time. When my dad wasn't there, she made me do things a child shouldn't even know about. When I did it wrong, she'd slap me and say, "Do it right."

I didn't know what *right* was. I didn't know what to do.

That feeling, of being totally lost, of not knowing what to do, felt worse than the abuse itself. In those moments with that woman, I made a promise to myself. I promised that I would never again find myself in a situation where I didn't know what to do.

Then, just a year later, my dad abandoned me and my baby sister at the hourly rate motel we had been living in. I was totally alone and didn't know how to take care of her. We had to leave and go outside when my dad's girlfriend, Amber, brought a trick back to the motel room. My sister, six months old, screamed relentlessly as I walked her up and down the motel walkway. Nothing I did calmed her down. I remember standing out back in the parking lot, staring at the road, willing my dad's car to appear. My baby sister cried, hungry, in my arms.

I was furious at myself. I had broken my promise. I had no idea what to do.

But that anger wouldn't help me figure out how to feed my sister. So I put it away. I figured out how to survive that day, then I figured out the next day, and the next. Eventually my dad came back.

As I got older, I could have gone back to that anger and gotten lost in it. I had every right to. I could have stayed bitter, resentful, and hurt. I could have replayed every moment of abuse, burning with the urge to hurt everyone who hurt me. I could have said *fuck you* to life and run away from it, with alcohol, drugs, or anything else that would let me escape.

I could have, but I chose not to.

I chose optimism. I chose gratitude. I chose to keep my eye fixed on the future I wanted for myself. I looked at the palaces in River Oaks and I chose to believe I could get there.

I chose to ask questions. Asking questions is my way of making sure I'll never break my promise to myself again. I'll never be in a situation where I don't know what to do.

How did I get there? I chose to.

I once read a story about twin brothers. One became successful in business and had a wife and three kids. His twin brother was addicted to drugs, robbed people, and was in and out of prison.

That brother was asked, "What led you to this life?"

He replied, "My father was an abusive alcoholic."

The twin brother who was successful was asked the same question.

He gave the same answer: "My father was an abusive alcoholic."

You can't choose what you were born into. You can't choose your childhood. You can't choose whether you're rich or poor. You can't choose the opportunities that will come your way. None of these circumstances are your choice, and none of them are your fault.

But they are your responsibility.

The choice I made each day to focus on the future, and to believe I could get there, was where Modern Leadership truly began for me. If I could get dealt the cards of my childhood and still choose to play the hand instead of fold, how many others could do the same? How much wisdom and talent could be unlocked by modeling the choice I made to get there?

Modern Leaders aren't born. They're made—by choice.

OPEN YOUR DOORS

What does it look like to open your doors?

Like all things Modern Leader, it's an action, not just an idea. But it's rooted in a concept that's important to understand. Just because the doors to your business have been physically open this whole time, just because you haven't been turning people away, doesn't mean your doors are truly open.

I talked earlier about how passive diversity initiatives don't work. The people outside the playbook filter *won't* simply appear at your door and walk through. You can't sit back and wait for people to come to you. If you do, I guarantee they will all have run the playbook to get there.

How do you open your doors to the JeVons of the streets?

First, ask yourself: what does an open door look like to a JeVon?

Take a look at your company website. How many people on your About Us page look like JeVon? If the answer is few to none, then you could be holding your doors open with both arms, but they would still look closed to JeVon. He knows that even if he managed to get in the room, he'd be the odd one out. He'd be a "what" instead of a "who". I've heard a similar sentiment from women I work with. If they look at a company page and they don't see many women, or they see zero women in leadership, they move on. Why invest your time in a company that hasn't invested time in people like you? That's a closed door.

Something else to look at is the way you list open roles. What qualifications are listed in your career descriptions? Would it be possible to get those qualifications without running the old playbook? If not, then that door doesn't just look shut to JeVon; there are triple locks on the door and bars on the windows.

What are the objectives of those qualifications you have listed? For instance, if one qualification is a college degree, ask yourself: what specifically are you looking for that a college degree gives a candidate? What would a different candidate *without* a degree be missing? (I'm not talking about professions like medicine, law, or engineering—those obviously require the advanced degree.)

In my experience, companies don't have great answers to those questions. If you keep drilling down, you'll get to a point where it's clear that they have *no* specific qualifications in mind. The college degree is being used as a filter, nothing more.

Can you name the top five qualities that will help a person be successful at your company?

If not, that's where to begin. Get clear on what you're looking for in additions to your company—characteristics about *people*, not their resumes.

I'll share mine: Creativity. Attention to detail. Accountability. Curiosity. Integrity.

From where I'm standing, a college degree isn't a measure or indication of *any* of those qualities. That's not to say that people who have a degree don't have those qualities—just that the degree isn't what proves that they do. In a world where parents can buy a fake high school history and test scores to get their kid into college, a college degree's usefulness as a measurement of character and hard work is pretty much zero, in my opinion. And no, that's not just because I don't have a degree; that's a fact.

If a degree is listed as a necessary qualification on our company's career descriptions, we're filtering out thousands of people who have years of demonstration in those qualities. We're also telling the world that our company is the kind of place where a piece of paper beats out demonstrated ability. If our company is willing to do that with a college degree, what other arbitrary measurements do we use to offer opportunities to people?

To JeVon, it's another closed door. That door might as well have a neon sign flashing a message: *Even if you can get in the room, you will not be welcome here. You will not belong.*

So, what does an open door look like?

An open door looks like any space where the people outside

the playbook filter can *see* themselves. It looks like a workplace that welcomes and celebrates every face, voice, and background.

To figure out what that is, you'll need to—you guessed it—ask questions. Ask people with diverse backgrounds what would attract them to your company. Find out what will signal to them that they won't just be tolerated and accepted, but welcomed and celebrated. Ask them to tell you their story, and ask how your company can fit into it. Listen. Learn. Seek to understand.

Modern Leadership is active, not passive.

Imagine a party where the host says, "Door's open, show up if you want."

Would you go to that party?

That's how I see the state of most diversity hiring efforts right now. There's an attitude of, "It's not our fault that they're not showing up."

No one shows up to a party they're not invited to.

An open door is an *invitation*.

HOW I GOT HERE ISN'T HOW WE GET THERE

I would love to know where Maria is today.

I'd want to ask her questions. I can only imagine the skills and insight a working single mom could bring to the table. There's so much I could learn from her, and back when we worked together in the mailroom, I was too focused on myself—and on staying in the room—to consider that she might have anything to teach me. I won't blame the playbook; I made the choice to run the ball down the field and leave her behind. I made the choice to slam the door shut behind me. I also won't apologize for that; it was the choice I needed to make at the time.

But now, I would choose to open the door and invite Maria in.

We have an opportunity in business today that hasn't existed until this moment. American society has never been so open to changing up the status quo, and the need to do so has never been so apparent. The future of business includes all voices, all backgrounds, all stories. We have an opportunity, and as Modern Leaders, it's our responsibility to execute on it.

We've opened our eyes. Now it's time to open our doors.

We can see everyone the playbook filtered out. They've been there all along. But the door is still closed. The old playbook is still the password for getting the door to open.

Rip up the playbook. Open your doors.

In the journey I've taken from a childhood of poverty to a career defined by the playbook to Modern Leadership, I've learned a lot about people. I've learned that everyone, *everyone*, has wisdom to offer. I've learned that a room that only includes a narrow slice of people isn't a room I want to be in, and a room that includes everyone is always going to have more energy, power, and service.

But what I've learned most in that journey is a truth about myself. I'm my own proof. I'm my own example for why Modern Leadership works.

I ran the playbook to get into the room, and I kept running it to stay there. But the greatest success I've had is when I turned to my own story to guide me, not the playbook. The hard-won insights from the training ground of my non-playbook life have provided the biggest business breakthroughs of my career.

One of the best compliments I ever received was from my boss when I was twenty-three, Mr. Gentry. One day he said to me, "Man, if I had eleven more of you, I could take over the world."

He wasn't referring to any talent I was born with. He was talking about how I chose to show up. How I paid attention, asked questions, and learned—and if there was no one to teach me, taught myself—what I needed to know to get there.

I ran the playbook. I left my name behind, and I got in the room. I left Maria behind, and I stayed in the room. I left my story behind and read the playbook aloud instead.

That's how I got there. But it's not how we move forward into the future.

I'm in the room now, and I made sure I can't get kicked out.

As a Modern Leader, I'll never close the door behind me again.

CHAPTER 5

REPARATIONS

I RECENTLY MADE THE DECISION TO LIST SCRIBE MEDIA as a black-owned business.

It's a move I had resisted for years, even though I own the controlling share of the company. Why should our business get extra credit just because I had a black father? It felt like taking a handout for something I had no control over. I didn't choose to be born mixed race (but I thank God I am).

I've always been uncomfortable with affirmative action. I spent my childhood on welfare. I often had to accept the charity of strangers for food and clothing. When you're forced to take handouts for basic survival, it comes with a lot of shame. It doesn't feel good to be on welfare; nobody wants a weekly check that reminds them they can't take care of themselves.

Side note: a fact that often gets edited out of the conversation on welfare is just how welfare breaks down demographically. Say "welfare", and it's common in our society for the conversation to focus on black people. But the truth is that, if you add up all the blacks and Latinos on welfare, it doesn't come close to the number of white people on welfare.

I worked so hard and sacrificed so much to get off the streets that any suggestion that I was given a leg up by affirmative action gets under my skin. I got where I am today on my own, thank you. That's been my attitude my entire adult life.

So when my race recently became a factor in an opportunity I won, I didn't know how to feel.

I was working to get a meeting with a large corporation that is notoriously difficult to get time with. The deal I intended to pitch them would mean millions for our company. I used to work in sales, and when I did, I was the best salesperson walking. I just refused to give up on a sale. I'd follow up as many times as it took; I'd come up with new and creative ways to get meetings and close deals. I drew on that background in going after this pitch meeting—I was not going to stop following up until I got in the room with the company's marketing team.

Finally, after knocking on a dozen doors for what seemed like months, I was on the phone with the right people who could make a meeting happen.

They asked me a question I wasn't expecting. "Are you a black-owned business?"

"Yes," I said, without really thinking about it. The question had taken me by surprise, and technically, we were.

The moment I said we were a black-owned business, the brick wall came down. Suddenly all their calendars were clear. Suddenly several different options for meetings were proposed to me. Deal terms were in the works.

I have to wonder what they would have said if my answer had been no, and I believe I know the answer.

The situation didn't sit well with me. As CEO of Scribe Media, I had a responsibility to the company to work for its success in every way I could. But what would that success mean if my race—something I have no control over—was the reason we got there?

On the other hand, I weighed the truth that the old playbook is an unbalanced playing field, and we still have a lot of catching up to do as a society. If this large corporation wanted to throw a few rocks on the other side of the scale by taking a meeting with me, is that perhaps a step toward progress that's greater than just me and the company I lead?

I know I'm not the only person who's struggled with questions like these. The emotions and opinions around programs like affirmative action are so varied person to person that it's impossible to form a consensus. I've known white people who staunchly support affirmative action, and I've known people of color who loathe the idea, and vice versa.

The same spectrum of opinions and emotions exists around an even more hot-button topic: slavery reparations. I'm always amazed at how heated discussions about reparations seem to get within a matter of seconds. The people who love the idea *love* it. And the people who hate it (me included) *hate* it.

Why do I hate it? For the same reason I'm uncomfortable with affirmative action. I've worked hard to earn everything I have. I don't want a handout or a "make right".

I've listened to every argument out there for why it's *not* a handout, it's owed, it's atonement, it's to level a hopelessly unequal playing field—you name it, I've heard it. I believe some of those arguments to be well-founded. I can understand why some people feel strongly that they want their due. I can acknowledge intellectually why the argument for reparations is logical. It doesn't make the idea any emotionally easier for me to swallow. If I ever get that check in the mail (unlikely), I'm sending it back certified mail with "Thanks, but no thanks" written in the memo line. And then I'll make a charitable donation of the same amount with my own money that I earned.

I don't speak for anyone but myself, and black America is

not a monolith of opinion. Others are strongly in favor of reparations. America's first black billionaire, BET founder Robert L. Johnson, is currently pushing a $14 trillion reparations proposal. From his point of view, it's the only way to make things right. The wide spectrum of beliefs on this subject is a good thing. We should be talking about subjects like reparations; we *should* be having discussions so deep we get emotional. Reckoning with our past is an American exercise that's long overdue.

What I believe is simple. There *is* no way America can make things right. We're not going to make up for 400 years of slavery, discrimination, and prejudice with one program, or one lump sum payment.

But that doesn't mean we do nothing.

We can't make things right. But we can stop making them *wrong*.

The Modern Leader understands that the choices they make in business have a direct impact on society, and that they have the power—and responsibility—to act.

That action doesn't need to be fixing everything all at once. It doesn't need to look like hiring less qualified candidates to meet a quota. And it doesn't need to look like a payout. I'm not invalidating those actions; they may have a place in our future. But in business, right this moment, we have an opportunity to make lasting change with every role we hire, every candidate we interview.

You can't offer everyone a job. But you *can* offer everyone a chance.

GETTING IN THE REPS

Let's take a look at two candidates for a role: Ashley and Shameka.

Ashley has been running the old playbook her entire life. She's grown up in a two-parent middle-class household. Her family isn't wealthy, but they're able to provide her with tutors so that she can make the grades that earn her scholarships, first to private prep school, and then to a Tier 1 university. Ashley also has a small college fund her parents had put away for her, so she doesn't have to work while in college to pay for room and board. Instead, she spends her spare time exploring various internships. Some are your basic grunt work, but some allow her to get a small foothold in the corporate world. Ashley's boss at her senior year internship, a VP of Marketing, becomes her mentor. By the time Ashley graduates with her degree, she already has several interviews for great jobs lined up.

When Ashley goes to these interviews, she's already had the experience of multiple years in corporate offices. She knows what to wear, what to say, and how to present herself. She knows what's expected of her, and she performs accordingly. Of three interviews, she only gets one offer—but it's a good offer, and she accepts. She begins her career at age 22.

Now let's look at Shameka. Shameka has grown up half with her mom, half in foster care. She's moved around a lot and has never been able to establish a network of friends. In the inner-city public schools she variably attends, Shameka keeps to herself and studies, knowing it's her only way out. But when it's time to apply for college, Shameka doesn't have the money for application fees. Even if she did, the idea of being able to pay for college tuition is a distant dream. Instead, she goes to community college for two years, paying for her classes with fifty hours a week at two different restaurants. She earns an Associate's degree in Accounting and uses this to start a book-keeping business, taking on a few small business clients in her neighborhood—dry cleaners, barber shops, and bodegas.

After building her client list for a couple of years, Shameka has earned enough to get an apartment on her own, and believes she has enough experience to qualify for corporate-level positions. She applies for a dozen roles, but none of them call her for an interview. Her lack of a Bachelor's degree has filtered her out of most hiring funnels. She applies for the role Ashley eventually lands; her resume gets a quick glance and even quicker dismissal from the hiring manager, who skims it looking for corporate experience and puts it aside when she finds none.

By the time Ashley and Shameka apply for the same job, Ashley has already had plenty of reps in corporate America. She's been immersed in the language of professionalism since her very first internship. She's been on dozens of job interviews; she's had practice. She knows how to perform in that environment.

Shameka, on the other hand, has had no practice. She's got no reps. She's by no means less qualified than Ashley when it comes to the skills needed for the role; if anything, she's *more* qualified. Her work ethic, personal responsibility, drive, and the results demonstrated by her successful business would be an obvious win for any company that brought her on board. But she hasn't been running Ashley's playbook. Ashley's playbook is full of drills for the big game. Shameka has been a free agent making up the plays as she goes along.

This is one of the main differences between JeVons from the streets and kids running the old playbook: getting in the reps. To get good at anything, you need opportunities to practice. For a lot of people, those opportunities are rare.

When I mentor young men from disadvantaged backgrounds, I spend a huge amount of time running drills with them, helping them get in the reps other kids who are running the playbook have naturally gotten to practice. Drills like: *make eye contact, extend your hand, and clearly say your full name.* Many of the kids I mentor have never given a real handshake in their lives.

Believe me, when someone has never given a handshake, you can tell. They stand out from the confident, firm handshakes—not in a good way. They radiate awkwardness and uncertainty. To a hiring manager, they don't seem like a sure bet.

I've learned in business that half of the time, no one is really listening to what you say. They're only taking in enough information to be reassured that you're confident in what you're doing.

If you can walk into a room and show that kind of confidence, it doesn't matter what raw skills you're bringing to the table. You're going to be taken more seriously than someone whose every look, word, and move makes it obvious that it's their first time in the room.

If the hiring manager at Ashley's company wasn't so conditioned by the old playbook, they might hold up the two resumes side by side and compare them purely based on demonstrated skills. They would see that Ashley has some experience in the kind of work environment they're hiring for, which is definitely a benefit; and they would see that she has a four-year degree. Looking at Shameka's, however, they would see experience in a variety of workplaces going back four years longer than Ashley. They would see time management and hustle in the jobs she juggled while getting her own degree—a two-year degree, but a degree just the same. They would see a successful entrepreneur who has been responsible not just for marketing, growth, finances, and customer service of her own business, but for the financial side of many clients' businesses as well. On balance, Shameka is bringing much more to the table when it comes to demonstrated skills. The only thing she lacks is the practice Ashley has had in the professional environment of corporate America. Shameka lacks what the old playbook specifically filters for.

When you remove the filter of the old playbook, people's backgrounds start looking a little different. Through the old playbook filter, Shameka looks unimpressive and unsuited to corporate work, a fish out of water. Remove that filter and look just at the basic facts of her experience and results, and you see a completely different picture.

A Modern Leader looks at a resume like Shameka's and sees opportunity. Yes, Ashley is a known factor. She's a sure bet. But Shameka has unique experience and is coming with a whole toolkit of demonstrated skills that may not look like the playbook, but might still offer phenomenal value to a corporation. A Modern Leader reaches out to Shameka, not with a handout, but with a chance. There's zero downside to offering Shameka an interview. The company has nothing to lose, and everything to gain, by offering Shameka the chance to get a rep in.

Offered just one interview, one shot at exposure to the corporate environment, a learner like Shameka is going to pick up some of the language and customs of the old playbook. Even if she doesn't get the job, she's going to have a better idea of how to get into the next room.

That's what opening your doors looks like. It's an invitation to the party. There are millions of talented people out there who could be the life of that party if they simply had an invitation.

COLLECTING TOKENS

Fact: most CEOs, HR heads, and corporate hiring managers *would* call the doors to their companies open.

And in doing so, they point at singular examples of diverse

hiring. In other words, they point to their token hires. They'll rattle off workplace demographic percentages, the numbers well-memorized and rehearsed. They've got a whole speech prepared to counter any criticism that might come their way about the inclusion, or lack thereof, in their workplaces.

That's what tokenism is all about: avoiding criticism. We're at a place in American society where business leaders fail to act until the jeers get too loud, the callouts too frequent—or the financial impact to their business too expensive.

Why does it take a threat to the bottom line for a CEO to do the right thing? So many business leaders are reacting, not acting. They're doing damage control, not solving problems. That's not Modern Leadership. From my perspective, that's not leadership at all.

Take the NFL's Washington Football Team (up until recently, the Washington Redskins). From as far back as the 1960s, the team had faced criticism of its name. Native American groups, the ACLU, major news organizations, even their own fans— seemingly everyone but the NFL and the team's owners and fans could agree that the name was offensive and outdated. The debate on this topic stretched six decades. That's sixty years of a company's leaders repeatedly being told their company name was flat-out racist, and those leaders taking no action besides vowing they'd never change the name.

Then George Floyd's murder happened. Ironically for a team with a famously insensitive name, a team that was the very last in the NFL to integrate black players, the Redskins posted a black square for Blackout Tuesday. I've already talked about how pointless I thought Blackout Tuesday was, but I had to laugh at the immediate roasting the Redskins received over social media for that tone-deaf move. Someone was asleep at the wheel on that one. Old playbook move.

Swept up in the tide of companies changing names and yanking syrup bottles off shelves, the Redskins name came under even hotter fire. Only this time, it wasn't just public shaming and cries of racism. This time, money was involved. Nike and FedEx threatened to pull sponsorships. Nike, Amazon, Target, and Walmart removed all Redskins apparel from retail sites.

It only took one day of their bottom line being threatened for Redskins leadership to initiate a "review" of the team name. By the end of the summer, the name was gone.

Sixty years of calls for leadership, and not one "leader" took action until money was at stake. That's sad.

Equally sad is any claim that the Redskins changing their name, or PepsiCo pulling bottles of Aunt Jemima off the shelves, does anything of substance for anyone outside the old playbook filter. Gestures like that are still tokenism. They're not change. They're not about people. They're about money, reputation, and avoiding the mob's pitchforks.

So are hiring quotas. You met your "diversity hiring percentage" for the year? Good for you—I guess that means you're done, right? Congratulations, you have a token minority to point to just in case anyone calls you out. "We hired a black woman as Chief Diversity Officer. We double-checked the box. Leave us alone."

Token gestures are pointless because they have nothing to do with people. They're focused on the company. They're not meant to open the door to invite more people in the room; they're meant to protect the people who are already inside. They're about preserving reputation and preventing criticism. Tokenism protects the old playbook by dressing it up in a socially acceptable costume. It is by definition a closed door.

I usually roll my eyes when I see a dictionary definition in a piece of writing, but the Merriam-Webster definition of *tokenism* is just too perfect. It reads: "The practice of doing something (such as hiring a person who belongs to a minority group) only to prevent criticism and give the appearance that people are being treated fairly."

Give the appearance that people are being treated fairly.

How about *actually* treating people fairly?

Leadership is about people, not appearances. A Modern Leader doesn't have time for token gestures. They're busy leading—and making actual change.

SHOW AND TELL

Like I discussed earlier, when I was growing up, the only options to get off the streets were to become a rapper or athlete. Or drug dealer, but that option just took me from the streets to prison.

It took until I was an adult to see that the athlete route wasn't even the ticket to freedom it seemed to be when I was hungry and dreaming in Dayton. Call it exaggerated, incendiary, or overblown, but the comparison between college sports and slavery has always rung true for me.

Earlier this year, on a podcast, I brought up that comparison. "The NCAA is the modern-day plantation," I said.

The host's jaw dropped. I wasn't the first or even the fifth person to publicly make the comparison, but apparently he'd never heard it.

"What do you mean by that?" he asked warily. I could tell he wasn't sure of his footing; he had the classic look I've seen on white people's faces that screams, *Am I allowed to talk about this?*

"Think about it. Young black men and women are put to work, and they're not allowed to get paid for it. They're literally out on the field doing physical labor for no pay. Meanwhile, the franchises and coaches are making millions. College coaches are the highest-paid public employees in most states. The athletes get nothing."

"They get a college degree," the host countered.

"Yes, they do. And then what?" I replied. "You think a Rayvonte or a Laquanda is getting a job in corporate America, even if they have a degree? The door is still closed. It's only open for the short period of time when their physical labor can make someone else money. Then it slams shut."

I gave that interview before the recent turn of events regarding the NCAA. As of July 2021, a student athlete can now make money from their name, image, and likeness, meaning they can take endorsement deals and profit from social media. It was a token gesture, in my opinion. Few kids are actually making an income off their likeness. And they're still not being paid for the work they're doing on the field, or getting a cut of the outrageous sums of money they're making for the franchises they play for—money made off of their backs.

Still, the door to the biggest payouts—high-level positions like head coach—is only barely cracked open. College teams may be predominantly black athletes, but their coaches are nearly always white. In 1981, the first black head coach of a college football team was hired, Dennis Green for Northwestern. And since then, less than 10% of top leadership positions in college football have been filled by black people.

When you zoom out like that, it's easier to see how the way we as a society have "opened doors" hasn't worked. I believe that one of the reasons tokenism prevails in corporate America is that business leaders choose to stay zoomed *in*. They're not looking at the big picture; they're reacting to each individual crisis with a hasty scramble to get society to stop yelling at them. They're not looking at the overall picture of what their company will look like in five years, ten years, or two decades; they're looking at this year's hiring and trying to hit an arbitrary number that "proves they care".

Looking at the big picture makes it clear that token gestures have little to no effect on the future.

So what does?

Simple: show and tell.

When I was a teenager trying to find a way off the streets, if someone had said the word "entrepreneur" to me I would have thought they were speaking another language. Now that I know what it means, I have and will continue to make sure that kids like me will know it, too.

When I get the chance to mentor youth about their potential, I use *show and tell*. My version is different than the version our kids are growing up with—there are no toys or pictures from the last vacation I took. My show and tell is about giving kids practice walking through an open door. It's about helping them get the reps in.

I show kids how to shake a hand and tell them why doing it the right way is important.

I show them what a financial advisor is and tell them how they can become one without a college degree.

I show them an example of attention to detail and tell them why it matters.

I show them a job application and tell them how to fill it out. Perhaps even more importantly, I tell them how to ask for one. You can tell a kid from the streets to go into Burger King for his first job, but if he doesn't know what to say when he walks in, he's not even going to get that application.

When my dad drove me through River Oaks and showed me those multi-million-dollar mansions, there was no *tell*. He didn't say a damn thing in the car ride. He didn't have to; just showing me opened my mind to what was possible in this life. And many years later, when I had the opportunity, I returned the favor.

I took forty kids from a halfway house on a field trip to the software company where I formerly worked. There they saw white boards full of code, conference rooms with massive screens, and computer monitors everywhere. We got them hooked up to play Madden in the conference room screens, ordered pizza, and ate in the breakroom that was stocked with free snacks and drinks.

They had the same look in their eyes that I knew I must have had that day in River Oaks. It was clear that they had never seen anything like that before. Hell, when we got on the elevator, it was the first time most of them had been on one before.

I showed them what was possible, and I told them how I got it. That was all—I didn't give any handouts, fill any quotas, or take up space that squeezed someone else out.

An open door looks closed until you can see what's on the other side. Modern Leadership is about opening eyes—not just yours, but everyone's. And it's about opening doors, not to an empty room, but to a future full of opportunity.

HIRE PEOPLE, NOT PLAYBOOKS

Some of the best performers I've ever hired don't have a college degree.

In fact, at Scribe Media, it's common for interviewers to walk into a room with a candidate completely cold, meaning they haven't seen the candidate's resume.

Why don't I look at resumes? Because hiring is about people, and a resume can't tell a person's story the way a curious conversation can.

I'm not suggesting that resumes are pointless. They have a purpose: they're used to categorize, compare, and filter people. They're meant to translate an individual background of experience into an easily digestible, easily organized format. They turn people into pages from the playbook. Then a hiring manager can stack, sort, and in some cases shred those pages without expending the time to consider the unique value of each person.

Of the best performers I've hired in my career, none of them listed what made them great on their resumes. They listed what's in the playbook template: education, references, work history, and so on. They translated themselves into a playbook page.

Imagine their confusion when I wanted to talk about *them*, not their resume.

In those conversations, I ask questions. I listen to their stories. I hear about everything they're bringing to the table that *isn't* on the playbook page. Like how their work ethic came from watching their parents struggle financially, and how they got a job as a teenager to help their family keep their home. Or how they launched their own business and learned the painful lessons of that business failing—but kept trying. Or how they're a single parent balancing advancing their career with the responsibility of caring for their child. These stories speak to me about creativity, accountability, results, drive, and integrity—all traits I value far more than degrees.

I've seen candidates get annoyed, even offended, when I won't look at their resume. In my experience, that's a red flag. Those candidates likely aren't bringing anything to the table *but* the playbook. They might even feel a little entitled to a certain consideration because of what school they went to or where they've worked. That entitlement earns a *no* from me. You're not entitled to anything just because you ran the playbook.

What demonstrated results have you achieved? What unique perspective and skill are you bringing to the table? What can you teach me? And what questions do you have for me? That's what I want to talk about in an interview.

Someone who didn't run the playbook or didn't have an invitation into the room has likely been passed over dozens of times over the years. They've watched candidates who are younger, less experienced, and less talented vault past them in hiring rounds simply because of the perfectly templated playbook page they can show. Offer someone without that playbook page a chance to shine in your organization, and I guarantee you they won't pass up the chance. They'll bring everything they have to their role. They'll shine brighter than most people with the perfect resume.

The playbook guides most corporate hiring because it reduces unknowns. Unknowns are dangerous. They're risks, and risks are expensive. Put aside that the greatest risks bring the greatest rewards—the unknowns that live outside the old playbook are only risks if you're looking through the playbook filter. Without that filter, they're no riskier than anyone else.

Look through the filter at Ashley and Shameka, and you see a proven model versus an unproven one. You see a college education and corporate training versus a self-employed service industry veteran. But remove the playbook filter, and suddenly the picture is much different. Now it's a contest between someone with high potential but few proven results, and someone with years of proven results and demonstrated success. The known and unknown swap places. Which candidate would you say is a riskier hire now?

I said at the start of this chapter that I'm not a fan of affirmative action. Well, here's the truth: the old playbook *is* affirmative action.

It's affirmative action for college-educated, economically privileged white men.

It uses a specific set of measurements to elevate one select slice of people over others, in order to create an environment that looks and performs a particular way.

The playbook may be proven, but it's proven for the past. Modern Leadership opens doors to the future.

CHAPTER 6

HOPE, WISH, AND LUCK

WHEN I WAS A KID, GOING DRIVING WITH MY DAD WAS something I looked forward to more than anything.

Did it involve witnessing crime, abuse, and often terrifying acts of violence? Did it mean I watched him beat up women more times than I can remember? Yes. But I was a kid who wanted to be with his dad. I didn't know any other existence.

I lost count of the times I sat in the window of my mother's apartment as a child, hoping my father would come pick me up the way he said he would.

Often, he didn't show up. All the hope in the world couldn't make my father keep his word.

I learned early on that hope got me nowhere.

There were too many times growing up that there was no food in our refrigerator, and I wished we had some so we didn't have to go to bed hungry.

It didn't work. Wishing didn't fill our bellies.

Starting out in my career, I'd see people more successful than me and think, "Man, they're lucky."

But they didn't get there by luck. And neither did I.

All the time, I see people complaining about their situation in life, wishing for things they don't have: a better job, a better car, more free time to relax, more skills and talent so they can make more money. Then they do nothing to get the things they wished for. It's as though they used up all their energy on the wishing part, and forgot to take action.

The language you live by is the life you create. Years ago, I eliminated the words "hope", "wish", and "luck" from my vocabulary. I had seen time and time again that those words were useless in actually getting what I wanted. In fact, they often detracted from the effort I was putting in. Hoping and wishing for things was time that could have been better spent working, asking questions, and studying business. And chalking other people's successes up to luck took away my responsibility for my own success. Luck meant that I had no control over my circumstances, that I was at the mercy of the universe rolling the dice. That didn't sit well with me.

Instead of hoping and wishing, I choose to *believe*. I believed I could get out of the hood and into River Oaks. I believed I could outwork everyone around me, and that hard work would distinguish me. I believed I could learn business well enough to one day be the CEO of a successful company. Betting on myself meant believing in myself, and believing in myself meant I had no choice but to take action and execute.

It's a formula I live by to this day.

Belief = Execution.

What I see across business leadership today isn't belief. It's hoping and wishing. The old playbook is breaking down; the structure of the business world is shifting. CEOs *hope* their companies will come out the other side intact. They *wish* for their luck to change.

As I write this book, we're two years into a pandemic disruption that has completely changed the face of business around the world. So many leaders are worried—and rightfully so—about how they're not only going to get through this, but what the future may hold for their business.

That kind of fear can be crippling. It leads to indecision, relying on luck. Hoping and wishing that their business will survive.

None of those things will get them through. *Belief* will. Execution will.

THE CHOICE IS YOURS

Every year when people start talking about their New Year's resolutions, I find myself asking the same question:

"Why wait until January 1st to start something? Especially something important or life-changing?"

I've never understood the concept of starting the new year strong. Why not start the next *day* strong? Start the next *hour* strong. Or, hell—start strong right now!

Your New Year's resolution is to stop smoking? If you woke up today at 6:55 a.m., stop smoking at 6:56. Why restrict yourself to a fictitious limit based on a made-up holiday tradition?

Why? Because it gives us a built-in excuse. It allows us to tell ourselves, *I know this cigarette I'm going to have today is bad for me, but it's okay because I'm quitting the first of the year.* You get to feel good that you made a plan, and meanwhile, you still get to smoke the cigarette. You get the false satisfaction of living into the future where you've already succeeded, while getting the real satisfaction of the present behavior you haven't changed.

We're afraid of taking that next step today because it means committing to something at which we might fail. We're not accountable to ourselves. In fact, if there's one area where our society is most lacking at the moment, in my opinion, it's accountability.

Everything is someone else's fault. Everything is "happening to" people, instead of the consequences of their actions. Everyone wants the freedom to make their own choices, but no one wants to acknowledge that their life is a result of those choices.

I modeled how I show up each day after Cecil, who was always "tremendous"—because as a black man in corporate America, he had to be. When people ask me how I'm doing, I tell them I'm "excellent". It's not lip service; I truly am excellent. If I'm ever *not* excellent, you can bet I'm already ten steps down the road to getting there.

If I don't like my circumstances, I change them.

It's not that simple, I hear from people. Bullshit. It is that simple. It may not be *easy,* but it really is that simple. It wasn't easy to get from the streets to River Oaks, but it was simple; I decided on what I wanted and I committed myself to getting there.

I've heard the same comment in countless interviews, podcasts, and Q&As. "Oh my God, JeVon, you had every reason to fail. You had every reason not to succeed."

I'd rather someone call me the n-word than say that.

My perspective? I had every reason *to* succeed. If you get through what I got through, there are no limits.

What these people are really saying is that if you're dealt a tough hand in life, it's totally fine for you to fold the game—to fail. They're saying that I would have been justified in sitting back and staying miserable on the streets. That if I'd given up, it would have been okay. Understandable.

Essentially, because of my background, I was given *permission* to fail.

This mindset makes no sense to me. It's giving up control of my future. There is only one thing in the entire world that I can fully control, and it's the choices I make in each moment. Why would I relinquish that control?

Accountability is acknowledging that the responsibility for your life lies with you, and you alone. Once you do that, all that's left to do is go after what you want.

I don't spend a lot of time on social media, but my wife, Megan, loves to scroll Instagram and show me what's happening out there in internet culture. One thing I notice is the frequency of work memes that worship Fridays and loathe Mondays. We've got an entire country of people who apparently spend all week white-knuckling and gritting their teeth until the weekend, when they drink, binge watch a TV show, doomscroll Facebook and Twitter, or all of the above. Then they wake up Monday morning filled with dread for another soul-sucking week ahead.

Why would you stay in a job you hate? Why would you trade

five days of misery for two days of, at best, a break from that misery, and at worst, a couch-bound recovery from it?

I hear people all the time wishing (there's that word again) they were rich. I've never heard any of them say they binge-studied the stock market all weekend. I've never heard of anyone binge-planning their financial future.

Accountability is an expression of control of your circumstances. Accountability is saying, *I'm accountable because I choose what happens to me. I get to decide what comes next.*

As a child, I didn't get to choose. As adults, we *all* have a choice.

Modern Leadership is a wholly accountable way of leading. The Modern Leader isn't at the mercy of anything; they embrace the power of their choices in creating the world they want to live in. They know no one is coming to save the day. They see a duty to act, and they see that duty as an opportunity to serve.

THE OLD PLAYBOOK DICTIONARY

I cringe when I hear company leaders talk about "training" their employees.

It's just one of many examples I come across daily of corporate language that puts people last, not first. When I hear "training", I think about teaching a dog to sit, stay, and fetch. The word means to embed an action or behavior so deeply in someone's brain that they act without thinking.

Do you really want people at your company who don't think?

I can hear the pushback now: *Of course I want people who think. It's just a word that describes learning how to do a job. It's not that deep.*

When I was a kid, I used to hear, "Sticks and stones may break my bones, but words will never hurt me." That wasn't my experience. When you get called half-breed and watch your mother get called a nigger-lover, the words hurt. I don't take words for granted, and I don't use them casually. Words *are* that deep.

If *training* is a word that describes learning, then why not just say that?

At Scribe Media, the word "train" isn't used. We don't train people, because people aren't dogs. We teach, coach, and mentor.

New tribe members don't do training; they do onboarding.

Learning a new role is just that: *learning*. Not training.

If the word "training" gets under my skin, then the phrase "human capital" is nails on a chalkboard. Coming from a childhood where I witnessed pimps use women as business assets, any language that paints people as objects disgusts me. The phrase "human capital" is so common and widely accepted that I see it everywhere from airport billboards to HR brochures to news articles on the economy. Every time I see it, I think of human trafficking.

If you see people as capital, take a step back and think about what that means about your company. Is it truly people-first, if people are seen solely as a way to produce profit? Are people just another asset on your balance sheet?

Again, I hear the pushback. *It's just a way of describing the value people bring to a business.*

Okay, sure. I ask again: why not just say that?

People *are* valuable to a business—in fact, without people, a business has no value. But humans aren't capital. There's no room for unique individuals in the definition of capital. Capital either produces profit or it doesn't.

The old playbook runs on a dictionary that separates people from business. It's based on profit first, people last. So much of this dictionary is casually dehumanizing in a way we've all just gotten used to. The old playbook paints a picture not of people, but of machines producing output. Not of a team working together toward a goal, but of automatons serving a superior authority.

None of this is surprising when you think about where American business saw its start. The management structures and work customs of American business were born in the institution of slavery, and its fingerprints are all over our business culture to this day.

You either own a company, or you "work for" it. Well, no one works *for* the company I serve; we all choose to work *with* the company. No one works "for me"; they work *with* me.

Companies "recruit and retain" employees. *Recruit?* That's how you raise an army. *Retain?* It sounds like holding someone prisoner. Dictionary entry for *retain:* "To keep possession of."

I don't want to "recruit and retain." I want to "offer and provide." I want to offer people an incredible company to come work with, offer them rewarding work, and provide an incredible culture for them to be part of.

Businesses define sweeping areas of operation as "low-level tasks". This is one I hear all the time among leaders who, in the same breath, will complain about the low ownership and accountability of the people at their company.

Ask yourself: if you define someone's work as low-level, why should they be motivated to do anything more than low-level work?

How dare you expect them to accept responsibility and perform at the highest level when you refer to their work as "low-level".

There are no low-level tasks. A task either moves the business forward, or it doesn't. If it does, it's critical. If it doesn't, why do it?

When people say "low-level," they're talking about a responsibility, duty, or task they don't value. Like taking out the trash. Janitorial work is seen as "low-level". Well, let the trash overflow for two weeks and see how low-level that task suddenly seems.

"Fail fast"? Why do I have to fail at all?

What I choose instead is the word "mistakes." We all make mistakes in life and in business. The goal is to learn, grow, and not repeat those mistakes.

I still remember when I first read that Thomas Edison said, "I didn't fail ten thousand times. I found ten thousand ways that didn't work." I thought to myself, *So that's the key: I just need to keep trying, no matter what.*

It became my mantra. *You only fail if you stop trying.*

I don't want to fail fast. I want to *learn* fast.

We're all accustomed to the old playbook dictionary. It's ingrained in our language, our culture, and our habits. Moving away from it means adding friction to our communication, and maybe it's this reason that keeps us using phrases like "human capital" without fully absorbing its dark connotation.

But we learned this language, and we can learn a new one. I know, because I wasn't fluent in the language of the old play-book; I had to learn it word by word.

Modern Leadership is writing a new dictionary with each action that puts people first. Modern Leaders understand that the people they serve are listening to each and every word they speak. Words have power beyond their surface meaning; they're the bricks that build our culture. Modern Leaders don't waste a single one. Every brick counts.

THE LANGUAGE OF MODERN LEADERSHIP

The language you use exposes how you think about people. You can't wish or hope for a Modern Leadership culture. It's your responsibility to build it brick by brick, starting with the words you use.

When's the last time you described the company you serve as "my people"? Said "my employees" or "my company"? Talked about people working "for" you?

No leader is any more important than anyone else in their organization, no matter what position they hold, and no leader is better than the people they are surrounded by.

And I do mean every leader—no matter what position.

I've worked in plenty of situations where leadership adopts the mindset that they sit above the people that make up the team. That creates an environment where people feel that their work is not as important or appreciated as the manager, the vice president, president, or CEO. Meanwhile, those leaders live for power. They create an environment where the team has to do what they say, regardless of whether or not it's the right thing, without question.

In the early days of my management career, it was difficult for me to wrap my mind around the idea of people working *for* me. I had a GED. I never felt like I was smarter than anyone else. As such, I wanted people to know that we were in this together. We were on the same level, whether someone had multiple degrees or none at all.

Leveling the playing field meant everything came down to results. How could we work *together* to accomplish our goals?

I've said it before, and I'll say it again—three letters behind your name does not make anyone a leader. Service to people is what makes someone a leader.

With that in mind, here's some new vocabulary for the Modern Leader:

It's not "your company", it's the company you serve.

They're not "your people", they're the people you support and lead.

The next time you hear yourself saying "I" and "my", consider changing it to "we" and "our". Unless you're owning a mistake— that's where "I" is appropriate.

No one works "for" you; they work with you.

With every word you say, tell the people you serve that the company is about *them*, not you.

Believe me, they're listening.

The words you use truly do create your reality. Modern Leadership has a distinct language. The Modern Leader's vocabulary doesn't contain *hope*, *wish*, and *luck*.

If you're hoping and wishing, you're not acting. If you're not acting, you're not leading.

Modern Leadership is a language of belief. Belief in the people we work with and that our ability to manage crises will see us through to the other side. Belief that we've surrounded ourselves with people far smarter than us who can navigate the inevitable pitfalls we're going to encounter. Belief that inviting everyone into the room will allow our businesses not only to survive, but to thrive.

Belief that with open eyes and open doors, we can create a business culture together that is built for the future, not the past.

Part Three

OPEN A BACKPACK

CHAPTER 7

FILL IN THE
BLANKS

"WHO NEEDS A PENCIL?"

It was my first day at a new school. As was often true when I was a kid, I was hungry; I would have to wait until the free welfare lunch to get a meal. I felt out of place next to the rest of the kids in the class. They all knew each other. They all had new clothes, new backpacks, and most importantly, school supplies.

I had nothing.

I felt my cheeks get hot as I raised my hand to signal that I did, in fact, need a pencil. The teacher passed one down to where I sat.

"And who needs a piece of paper?" she asked next.

I raised my hand again.

Next to me, a kid named Johnny opened up a pristine new Spider-Man backpack, took out his pencil and paper, and glanced at me. I couldn't tell if his look was disgust, pity, or both, but I know how it made me feel.

From the perspective of the adults looking at school attendance rates, I had already achieved their objective: I was in school. My butt was in my seat.

But was I prepared? Did I have what I needed to succeed?

Not even close.

In order to get those things, I had to stand out. I had to be the kid who raised his hand while everyone else waited.

I was there, but just being there wasn't enough. Every other kid walked in that September morning with a new backpack full of the supplies they would need to learn. By walking in with nothing, I was already behind the rest of the class. I was already at a disadvantage.

This memory comes to mind often. All the time, I notice situations where people "get there"—but don't have what they need to be able to *stay* there. As a society, we talk about education, but not preparation. We talk about tolerance, but not welcoming. We talk about diversity, but not understanding.

Modern Leadership doesn't stop once you've opened your eyes and opened your doors. You're now seeing the people the old playbook previously filtered out. You've invited and welcomed them in.

Now it's time to extend the tools they need to thrive.

It's time to open a backpack.

EVERYONE IS MISSING SOMETHING

When I talk to other business leaders, the discussion often turns to employee perks.

Depending on your mindset, employee perks are either a great investment or an unreasonable burden. What I've found interesting is how many CEOs *say* it's a great investment, but the way they talk about employees actually *using* the perks says that they're in the "burden" camp.

They say it in subtle ways. There will be a quick joke cracked about how many women on their payroll are currently pregnant and have upcoming maternity leave. Or a comment like, "When I was starting out, nobody gave *me* flex time and education benefits."

Well, sure they didn't. Someone who came up in the old playbook doesn't need education benefits. They already have all the education they could ever want, likely paid in full. That's what got them through the playbook filter in the first place.

The old playbook is a closed loop. People who make it through the playbook filter do so because they already have what they need to thrive in a playbook culture. They already fit in, and they already have all the tools necessary to be able to devote all their energy and attention to succeeding. They don't *need* perks.

People who don't fit the old playbook likely don't have what they need to stay "in the room" if they make it there. Even if they've been seen, invited, and welcomed in, their position is still shaky. Everyone else has a Spider-Man backpack, and they don't even have a pencil and a piece of paper. They're behind, right out of the gate. And without those tools, they're unlikely to catch up.

I've listened to CEOs griping about having to "bend over backwards" for certain employees who are "missing" the tools other employees (as in: playbook-raised people) already bring with them.

I challenge that viewpoint. Because, yes, the single mother of two kids might be "missing" the completely clear schedule that would allow her to be available around the clock.

But the other employees are missing the unique experience and perspective that a single mother brings to the table. In ways the old playbook often minimizes as "being green" or "learning the ropes", those other employees are having to fill in blanks on responsibility, accountability, commitment, and life experience that the single mother brings with her.

Everyone is missing *something*. But the old playbook tells us that certain things are "normal" to be missing, while other things constitute a burden.

Ask yourself: how many incredible people are you *not* working with right now, simply because they don't have the tools they need to thrive in your organization?

How many people in your organization are constantly having to raise their hand for a pencil and piece of paper?

What if, instead, you handed them a backpack full of supplies the moment they walked through the door? What if the stress and isolation of constantly not having what they need, constantly worrying about being behind, simply evaporated?

How much happier would the people in your company be?

I often imagine what my school life would have been like if I'd been handed my own Spider-Man backpack full of school supplies right when I entered the classroom. Having everything I needed to succeed would have been amazing. Without having to worry constantly about what I was going without, or how I was behind, or things I didn't understand, I would have had the freedom to just *learn*.

Given those tools, and free to focus on learning, I actually believe I would have been a great student. I recently learned about the *cum laude* system in higher education, and I believe I would have graduated college *summa cum laude*. I believe I would have excelled at school the same way I went on to excel at setting sales records.

The Modern Leader doesn't ask what they "have to" provide for the people they serve. They don't look at employee resources and benefits as a counterpoint to their bottom line.

Instead, they ask themselves: what *more* can we be providing? What can we take off people's plates to make more room for learning, innovating, and creating?

They ask questions. They get to know what the people they serve are bringing to the table, and they proactively fill in the blanks of anything that's missing.

Because everyone is missing *something*. Why not ensure to the best of your ability that everyone is missing *nothing*?

AN UNTAPPED EMERGENCY FUND

Several years ago, I read a statistic that forty-five percent of Americans don't have a spare $400 in cash in case of an emergency.

It shocked me, but it didn't surprise me. I had lived half my life not just paycheck-to-paycheck, but more like paycheck-to-*last month's*-paycheck. Every dollar was already spent before it was earned. The idea of having money set aside for an emergency didn't exist in my upbringing. If we had money, it bought us food or turned the lights back on.

As a former poor child, when I read that statistic, I felt it deep in my gut. As a business leader, it rang alarm bells in my head.

Forty-five percent of Americans not having $400 in case of emergency constituted a threat to the organization I served as CEO.

Even adjusting for the fact that, as a publishing company, there was a certain degree of old-playbook filtering in the people who applied to come work with Scribe, there was still a strong likelihood that a quarter or more of the Scribe tribe didn't have $400 cash in case of emergency.

I remembered the stress and fear of worrying about money. I remembered the way all my mom and I could focus on sometimes was figuring out where our next rent payment would come from, or if we would eat that night.

What if we could remove that stress, fear, and worry for the Scribe tribe?

At the next company summit, with the entire company in the room, we announced a new benefit. Scribe would provide a $1500 no-questions-asked emergency loan to any tribe member who needed it. The cash would be in their bank account the same day, and the repayment plan would be individually determined based on the tribe member's needs. They didn't even need to provide an explanation. The money was simply there if they ever needed it for any reason.

When this was announced, I watched the faces of the tribe. People looked awestruck. Some looked like a weight had been lifted. Even if they didn't need the money at that moment, the removal of worry, stress, and fear was like a breath of fresh air.

I received messages of gratitude from tribe members.

I'm fortunate to be confident I'll never need to tap the fund, but just knowing it's there is incredible.

This is huge for me. Now I know if anything happens, I'm safe.

"Safe" was a word that came up often when tribe members talked about the emergency fund. It gave them a feeling of safety and security.

It's been four years since we put the emergency fund in place. We have over one hundred people working at Scribe.

Want to guess how many times it's been tapped?

Three.

That's right. For the grand total of $4,500 over four years—all of which was repaid—Scribe was able to create a relationship of safety and security for every person within the organization. That safety made room for people to think, create, learn, collaborate, and innovate. It made room for happiness.

That's priceless. And a great way to "allocate capital".

As a Modern Leader, when you read that nearly half of Americans don't have $400 cash for emergencies, you understand that you have a responsibility to do something about that.

I've heard arguments that people should be accountable for their own finances. That they should have planned better, spent less, sacrificed more. That no one is responsible for their situation but themselves, and they need to take accountability.

Those arguments are copy-pasted from the old playbook mindset. The old playbook tells us that it *should* be easy to have an emergency fund of our own, and that anyone who doesn't just isn't working hard enough.

The fact is, we don't have any idea why someone might not have $400 cash saved for emergencies. We don't know where their starting line was, we don't know what choices they've had to make, and we don't know what circumstances they've faced. Things seem simple when you look through the old playbook lens: *Of course you can save $400. You just spend less and put more in the bank.* But life for those outside the playbook lens often isn't that simple. And it's one of the reasons those people get filtered out. Everyone has a story; don't judge what you haven't read.

If you take the attitude that these people get their paychecks, and you aren't responsible for anything else, then don't be surprised when they quit. Don't be surprised that they don't give you a hundred percent effort or go the extra mile. But when you go the extra mile, they'll go the extra mile.

The Modern Leader has opened their eyes. They've opened their doors. They know how to listen, learn, and seek to understand. Now they're constantly looking for supplies to put in the backpack. They understand that the success of the organization depends on people having the tools they need to advance that success.

A Modern Leadership culture fills in the blanks so that everyone has what they need.

SMALL PEBBLES, BIG RIPPLES

I know the word "responsibility" sounds heavy.

And many leaders, whether they admit it or not, pass responsibility off to others.

When you look at the concept of opening a backpack from a bird's eye view, it can seem too big to get a hold of. So many people are missing so many things they need. How can you balance responsibility to the people you serve with the reality of what you can reasonably accomplish?

This is where I ask you to let go of the big picture.

You can't do everything all at once, and if you tried, you'd get nowhere. I see other business leaders get stuck on this point; they can't fix *everything*, so they freeze, and do *nothing*.

Zoom in. *Way* in.

Start with one person. It can be anyone in your organization. You've talked to them; you've asked questions and sought to understand them. (And if you haven't, start there.)

What might they be missing? What might you be able to fill their Spider-Man backpack with?

It doesn't even have to cost money. To someone who's never been seen or respected by a company leader, a simple "hello" can be a Spider-Man backpack.

The key is to zoom in. Consider individuals, and the unique ways you might be able to enable each individual's safety, happiness, and success. For each individual need you identify and find a way to provide for, I guarantee you there are a dozen more people who are missing the same thing. You have the opportunity to create huge effects throughout your entire company just by zooming in on one person's needs.

This isn't charity. The Modern Leader understands that they have a clear business interest in giving people in their company everything they need to succeed—everything they didn't walk in there with.

Maybe they walked in with a backpack, but no supplies.

Maybe they walked in with a Spider-Man backpack and a few pencils, but no paper.

Maybe they walked in with nothing.

Zoom in. Focus on one person. How can you increase their feeling of safety? What burden can you take off their shoulders? What more can you provide?

It's tossing one pebble into a lake, but it makes ripples that travel across the entire surface.

Years ago, at Headspring, we started a backpack drive for local schools. We asked for donations of backpacks full of school supplies, and for every backpack that was donated, we matched it. By the time the drive was done, we'd collected 2,000 backpacks full of school supplies. Lone Star Overnight, the FedEx of Texas, donated their vans to load up the backpacks and make deliveries.

That's an example of something you can do right now. It doesn't cost all your time. It doesn't even cost much of your money. Does it fix the problem of lack of resources in American schools? No. Did it fix one particular problem shared by 2,000 Texas kids one year? *Yes.*

Small steps add up to big moves. Zoom in.

When I came to Scribe, I brought with me the idea of the backpack drive. But this time, we decided to zoom in even further. We put together a list of the ten Austin schools with the highest percentage of students in the free lunch program. As a new startup, we didn't have the funds to make a difference for all those schools. We were at a point in our company history where I was watching the cash flow like a hawk day by day. We couldn't provide 2,000 backpacks like we'd done at Headspring.

So, instead, we zoomed in. "Which school is closest to us?" I asked.

It turned out that one of those schools was just four blocks away from our office.

At the start of the school year, every kid at that school got a backpack with the full supply list that they needed. It was a fraction of the amount we'd been able to provide at Headspring, but it made a difference for one school of 400 kids. And with each of those kids provided for, how much more would they focus on learning? How much safer and taken care of would they feel?

A Modern Leadership culture is one of *action*. Even if that action is zoomed in just to one person.

By providing for that person, you're enabling them to think, create, and innovate. You're offering a relationship of safety. You're creating a ripple effect throughout everyone else in the organization—that safety and freedom to thrive will impact everyone.

Most importantly, you're ensuring that no matter what they walk in the door with, each person who is welcomed through the door you've opened has the tools they need to help take the company into the future.

CHAPTER 8

DIVERSITY HAS NO FINISH LINE

WHEN I WAS TWENTY-THREE, I MOVED OUT TO PORTLAND, Oregon to run three offices for my first boss, Mr. Gentry. Full of pine trees and fresh air, the Pacific Northwest was nothing like Dayton. I felt like I'd won the lottery. I settled down in a suburb called Lake Oswego. It was a picturesque town full of the kind of perfectly cut lawns I remembered from my drive through River Oaks.

I soon realized, though, that Lake Oswego was empty of something else: *anyone* who looked like me.

Locals called it "Lake No-Negro".

I didn't much care. For the first time in my life, I had money in the bank and a great job that had no danger of disappearing. I felt secure, safe, and prosperous. I wrote in *I Got There* about the time I got racially profiled driving my Jeep Grand Cherokee in Lake Oswego, and how if anything, it only spurred me to work harder. I had money, and money had bought me a ticket to the neighborhood. No one could take that away.

It felt great—until one day when I found out that just making it into the neighborhood wasn't enough. Money had bought me a ticket in. But it couldn't buy being welcomed.

I had stopped one morning before work at a fancy coffee shop near my house. Not like a Starbucks; I'm talking a local place, the kind of coffee shop where they do pour-overs and have single origin beans on display.

The kind of coffee I was used to drinking came pre-ground from a plastic canister. I'd never had espresso before. As I stood looking up at the menu on the wall, I realized that I didn't know what any of the words meant. I didn't know what the drinks were or what was in them.

When I got up to the front of the line, I said, "I'll have a medium *lattie*."

The barista, a white woman not much older than me, looked at me like I was an idiot.

"You mean a *lah-tay?*" she said loudly, the pronunciation exaggerated. People waiting for their drinks nearby turned and looked over at us.

Getting pulled over for driving while being black hadn't thrown me. But for some reason, this coffee moment did. That was the moment I realized that no matter how much I edited myself, no matter how much of my story I erased, I still stood out. I was still the mixed-race kid who at times wasn't welcomed in either world.

It's funny how such a small moment stands out in my memory. The language of the old playbook was one I had to learn day by day, question by question. It's one I'm still learning.

You can open your doors wide, you can create a culture everyone can see themselves in, and you can offer people the opportunity to interview for a role regardless of their background. You can do all that, and the door still isn't open.

That moment was almost thirty years ago. When I look around today, the doors to corporate America are still just as closed.

It's not new. It hasn't changed. And, despite decades of "diversity initiatives" being a front-and-center hot topic in nearly every business conversation, despite countless billions of dollars spent on trying to create a more inclusive workplace, we've got very few actual *results* to show for it.

Why?

OUR CHOICE

"While it might sound like an excuse, the unfortunate reality is that there is a very limited pool of black talent to recruit from."

Believe it or not, that isn't a quote from the 70s, 80s, 90s, or even 2000s.

That's Charles Scharf, CEO of Wells Fargo, in the year 2020. He wasn't the only public figure to put his foot in his mouth that year, not by a long shot. 2020 was a year that saw many leaders across business and government being publicly called upon to apologize for "insensitive remarks."

Well, I don't call what Charles Sharf said an "insensitive remark."

I call it the typical mindset straight out of the old playbook.

Mr. Scharf did publicly apologize, and Wells Fargo committed to doubling its number of black leaders over five years, as well as tying executive compensation to achievement of its diversity "goals". Anyone would probably agree that top leadership at Wells Fargo will be aggressively working on its diversity initiative, being that their salary and bonuses are tied to its success.

My question is, what happens once they meet those goals?

Here's what I predict. Those old-playbook executives will get their payout for checking the "diversity" box. Everyone will pat themselves on the back for hitting their hiring quotas. The heat of public attention will have died down considerably by then, and company leadership can breathe a sigh of relief that they're probably not going to get called out again anytime soon. And if they do, they have a "successful" diversity initiative to point to. Company attention focuses elsewhere. *Diversity? We finished that. What's next?*

Meanwhile, Rayvonte still isn't in the room. He didn't make it anywhere close to the door.

That's how it's gone in corporate America for nearly half a century. Diversity "initiatives" *don't work.*

If the diversity initiatives companies have been running for thirty years actually *did* work, then why do we still see such massive racial inequity in top corporate positions? Why are only forty-one of the Fortune 500 CEOs women? Why are only five of them black?

If diversity initiatives worked, why did I need to change my name in order to get in the room?

Recently, on LinkedIn, a fellow CEO commented a phenomenal phrase on one of my posts.

What you are not changing, you are choosing.

This phrase is what I keep coming back to when it comes to diversity initiatives. Study after study has shown that they don't work. That they've barely made a dent in the racial and gender disparities that still define America's business world. Despite all the attention, public callouts, editorials, corporate trainings, affirmative action, and quotas…for the most part, corporate America has not changed.

What we're not changing, we're choosing. At this point, our lack of diversity is *our choice*.

It's a choice that doesn't surprise me. After all, the old playbook is written on a foundation of putting people last. Diversity is *people*, pure and simple. So putting people last is the same thing as putting diversity last.

The old playbook sees diversity as a box to check off, a task to complete. But the Modern Leader knows that they'll *never* be done with diversity. Because diversity isn't an initiative. Diversity is a culture you live, not a project you finish. Bringing all people together is the foundation of any great business. Companies that see diversity as an initiative with a start and a finish and reports and metrics aren't putting people first, and they won't survive the changing business environment.

Modern Leadership isn't about quotas. It's not about checking a box.

As a Modern Leader, you'll never be "done."

You'll never "meet the goal."

There is no goal.

Because diversity has no finish line.

HAVE THE CONVERSATION

I can't count the number of times I've been the only person of color in an all-white boardroom.

When I am, and the discussion turns to issues of race in the workplace, take one guess who everyone turns to look at.

This is a common experience among people of color, if the dozens of people who have shared that experience with me is any indication. When you're the token minority, you're suddenly the sacred keeper of all minority knowledge and wisdom. People spend years and tens of thousands of dollars to get PhDs in African American Studies, but apparently all I had to do was show up as mixed race in a room full of old-playbook faces!

When we're interviewing candidates at Scribe, we pay close attention to every detail of the interviews. We notice the little things. Something we've noticed is that one of our tribe members, a young black woman, is often the only one who gets questions about the company's diversity efforts. It's an immediate red flag for us—those candidates are likely not culture adds.

Diversity isn't a Black issue. It isn't a Hispanic issue. It isn't a female issue or an LGBT issue.

Diversity is about people. It's on all of us, together, to put people first. It's our choice.

If the only people you're talking to about diversity are people of color—if the topic never comes up at all unless there's a minority in the room—that's the old playbook at work. The old playbook tells us that the default is straight, white, male, college-educated, and that anything else is "other". The old playbook tells us that diversity is something you have to *do*, not something you choose to live by simply putting people first.

These days, companies have put even more distance between leadership and diversity by hiring Chief Diversity Officers, or CDOs. It's odd to me that this is seen as a move *for* diversity; if anything, now the leaders are off the hook!

These CDOs often wind up being the token minority in an old-playbook company. They're brought in to "fix the diversity problem", often in response to a public outcry of some kind— the summer of 2020, following George Floyd's murder, saw the peak of the over 100% increase in CDO hires since 2015. And yet, according to many of these professionals, what they face once they're hired is anything but encouraging. In fact, they spend most of their time trying to convince company leadership that diversity and inclusion are important. Somehow, they're responsible for making the business case for the very thing they were hired to do. Turnover in these roles is on the rise; the average CDO tenure is just three years.

Is that any surprise? People of color finally get in the door, and it's just to cover the gaps in knowledge the old-playbook leaders have about diversity. That doesn't feel good. Even in a C-suite role, their otherness defines them.

Meanwhile, the rest of the C-suite doesn't have to actually think or talk about diversity anymore. They hired someone whose job it is to do that thinking for them. All they have to do is wait for their CDO to tell them what to do next—but in so many instances, they don't listen, and they don't actually care.

That's not responsibility. That's not accountability. That's not Modern Leadership.

If you've opened your eyes and opened your doors, fantastic. But when the people outside the old playbook lens get inside, what are they hearing you say? Are you leaving the conversation about diversity to them, and them alone? How much trust can possibly be built by leadership when the impression given is that diversity only matters to people of color?

If you're following, you're not leading. The old playbook may not be your fault, but it's your responsibility to change it, rip it up, and throw it away. Diversity has no finish line. And neither does leadership.

Is the conversation about race in the workplace uncomfortable?

Yes. It brings up old wounds. It pulls front and center the reality of our history. But avoiding the conversation hasn't worked, and it's time to face it head on.

Why are we all so terrified of discomfort? We're capable of more than this.

Have the conversation. Or, even better: *start* the conversation.

CALL IT WHAT IT IS

In all the empty gestures I saw as companies flailed in the wake of George Floyd's murder, there was one trend in particular that summed up for me everything wrong with the way we talk about diversity in business. It wasn't new, but it was amplified due to the increase of attention on the subject.

People in business were talking about diversity more, but they had stopped using the word "diversity".

Instead, they'd come up with cute acronyms that stood in for the word. D&I. DEI.

Everywhere I turned, every think piece and article, every podcast, every news anchor, even the front page of our PEO provider's website—they all started using these acronyms. I noticed that candidates who came in to interview with us parroted these easy terms when asking about our company's culture.

Sure, you could say that it's just faster and easier to rattle off an acronym. But from my perspective, that's not the whole story.

When I heard people start saying "DEI" in place of the word

"diversity", it reminded me of how politicians had stopped using the phrase Black Lives Matter, and started referring to it as simply "BLM". It was easier to hide behind the acronym than to say the words aloud. To actually *say* the words "black lives matter" meant being confronted with the weight of what they meant. Much easier to avoid that discomfort with the mask of an acronym.

I started pushing back when I heard "DEI" or "D&I". Whenever I heard one of the acronyms, I'd ask questions.

What exactly does DEI mean to you?

What are you really asking about? People of color? Women? Gays?

What conversation are you trying to have?

Most of the time, this led to me watching people scramble for an answer they didn't have. It seemed to me that to most people the details behind the acronym didn't really matter. What mattered was that they had said the magic acronym that proved they cared. They'd been given a buzzword to use to signal their virtue. For the most part, I wasn't finding a lot of critical thinking happening behind the safety of that buzzword.

That's the problem with the old playbook: it's cynical.

The old playbook demands a "business case" for diversity and inclusion. It demands a profit from respecting the humanity of others. It characterizes diversity as an initiative, as a project a company takes on to achieve a goal. At best, and least commonly, that goal is a true commitment to a wider base of perspective. At worst, and much more of the time, the goal is better optics.

No one wants a company About Us webpage that's all white men…but only because it *looks bad*.

The old playbook guides us to do just enough for people that the company "looks good", or at least doesn't look quite as bad as its competitors. The priority isn't moving the needle. It's avoiding being called out.

What would it look like if diversity wasn't an initiative, but rather something you *lived*?

That's how the Modern Leader sees their role.

If you're a CEO, a leader, or a future Modern Leader, I have a challenge for you.

Stop using acronyms like DEI.

Stop hiding behind the easy mask.

Call it what it is. Diversity. Equity. Inclusion. *People*. All people.

Yes, saying these words shines a light on the fact that your company might be lacking in these areas. But you know what? So are most companies. This has been our choice. It's a choice we're all reckoning with together.

And together, we can choose what we do next.

CHAPTER 9

A MODERN LEADER CODE

IF YOU DO RIGHT, YOU GET RIGHT.

This is a phrase I repeat to myself daily. I also repeat this to any person in a leadership position, or anyone learning how to develop into a leader.

Being a leader is largely about making decisions. When I think about the unique skill I bring to the table as the CEO of Scribe, it doesn't look like the specialized expertise of the top-level writers, editors, designers, technical professionals, client experience architects, and operations directors I'm surrounded by. In fact, when it comes to pure credentials, I have among the fewest in the entire company.

The unique skill I bring as CEO is simple: I make decisions. I surround myself with people far smarter than myself, I ask questions, I listen to the experts, I weigh all the factors on the table, and I make what I believe is the best decision.

I read once that a CEO's role is simple. As the leader of a company, you're a decision engine. You might hold expertise in certain areas, but *being* the expert isn't your role. Your role is to put the right experts in the right seats, listen to them, and make the final decision.

Success in my role at Scribe doesn't look like a beautifully designed book cover or a high-return marketing campaign. It looks like making decisions correctly. It looks like the dozens of decisions I make daily leading the company closer to growth, profit, and the fulfillment of our mission: unlocking the world's wisdom. And above all, it looks like putting people first.

If I look around at the state of leadership in corporate America, it strikes me that there's one huge blind spot in most high-level decision-making. If you've read this far, you can probably guess what that blind spot is.

Say it with me: *people.*

Leaders are *very* adept at making decisions for other people—and yet much of the time, those decisions don't actually benefit those people.

Leaders are apt to say things like, "I speak for the voiceless." "I'm a megaphone for *x group*." "I'm advocating for those who can't advocate for themselves."

I prefer to let people speak for themselves. Believe me, they're perfectly able to do so. In fact, they *do*. They have been speaking for themselves this entire time. *We* haven't been hearing them. The old playbook has been blocking out their voices like noise-canceling headphones.

When did leadership become all about the leaders themselves, and not the people they serve?

I believe there's a key element missing from leadership culture. We're missing a code of values.

Leaders have been operating from a playbook that was written to put profit first, not people. We already know that playbook won't work anymore.

But as leaders, what are we left with?

Modern Leadership offers a new code of values, but it won't be handed to you. Like I said earlier in this book, Modern Leadership isn't a playbook.

Following a playbook is just that: *following*. You're not a leader if you're following.

Your first step into Modern Leadership is to develop your *own* code.

To lead, you have to make decisions. You have to decide: what matters to you?

What defines your leadership?

What are your leadership values?

What is your Modern Leader code?

I shared at the beginning one defining value of my own Modern Leader code: *if you do right, you get right.* I'm going to share in this chapter the values that make up my personal leadership code.

PEOPLE

At Scribe, we pride ourselves on our Culture Bible. It's our own company code of values, and it represents a commitment from each of us to live by and uphold those values. The Culture Bible was originally written by our two co-founders, but they specifically didn't want to set it in stone like the ten commandments. They intended it to be a living, breathing guide that would be consistently reconsidered and revised as the company grew.

And that's just what we've done. Our Culture Bible has always lived online as a public-facing document open to discussion and comment. Those who have been following Scribe from the early days have seen major changes to our Culture Bible over the years.

The biggest change came about in the company's third year.

Originally, our Values were in a different order. The top Value was Results. The second Value was People.

When I became CEO, I decided to shift that. To me, it was a no-brainer that our company's #1 Value was, and always would be, People.

We put people first. We do right by people. The decisions we make move us closer to many outcomes, but those outcomes *always* involve what is best for people—*all* people.

When I was coming up in business, I saw examples of leadership that did put people first, but it wasn't *all* people. It was usually *one* person. The leader.

I wondered: was there a basic fact about leadership that in order to lead, you had to enrich yourself first, others second?

I didn't know the answer, but I knew I didn't want to live my life that way. When I began rising in the ranks of leadership, I made myself a promise: if I ever found myself making decisions that benefited myself before benefiting others, I would step down and resign.

Leadership isn't about you.

If you're in leadership, 99.99999 percent of the decisions you make should *never* be for you or for your benefit. If you find yourself in a leadership position and are making decisions for yourself, resign. Every decision that you make should be for the greater good of the people that you serve. That's why you're in the role—not to wield power, have control of decisions, or get a huge bonus at the end of each year.

As a leader, you're responsible to the people that you serve. And you're only a leader if those people allow you to lead. If you're in a leadership position and the people you're leading don't like you and you're not serving the people you're leading, that's called being a dictator, not a leader.

CURIOSITY

One of my favorite conversation-starters is, "What one word that describes your life do you want written on your tombstone?"

My answer is *Fair*. I want to be remembered as someone who weighed the needs of everyone, and promoted an environment of fairness and welcoming to all.

That said, if you asked most people who work with me, live with me, or have met me, you'd probably get a different answer.

Ask questions.

I say that one phrase more than probably any other. I say it so much that I've heard people cut me off before I start and say it *for* me.

That's fine by me. If I'm known for being a little repetitive, at least it's an idea worth repeating.

Asking questions is, to me, the ultimate act of putting people first. When you ask people questions, it signifies that you want to hear their perspective. That you don't believe you know everything already. That you want to gain knowledge that will enable you to serve them better. That you want to simply *know* them.

One thing I've found to be true in my time is that *all* of us want to be known. We want to be seen authentically for who we are, and welcomed as our truest selves. We want to be celebrated for the uniqueness that we bring to the table.

As a leader, if I'm not asking questions, I'm subtly building a culture that says the opposite of all that. I'm building a culture that says, "Your ideas aren't needed. I already know everything. I don't care what you think or have to say. I don't care about *you.*"

If you're not curious, then in my opinion, you're not leading. You're elevating yourself, and that's a very different thing.

Leadership isn't *above*. It's *ahead*. As a leader, you don't sit at the top of an organization; you sit out front. You're the first to see what's coming. You're the one to take the hits before they can impact everyone else. Your job is to see into the future, make decisions, and lead everyone else there.

You can only do this by asking questions *constantly*. The day you wake up and know everything is the day you should resign.

SERVICE

I didn't always feel strongly about devoting my career to serving others. In fact, much of my early career in sales was spent doing everything I could to get ahead of others. I was out to get mine no matter what. The classic salesperson vs. the rest of the company stereotype? That was me. "I sold it, so you'd better figure out how to make it." I look back and wince a little at how self-centered I was chasing personal wealth over serving the company of people I worked with.

This changed when I began to take on positions of leadership at Headspring, and I saw the culture a "get mine" philosophy created. Businesses don't go very far when everyone is out for themselves. In my experience, any truly great company culture is based on Service. Serving each other, serving customers, and serving the mission.

I now hold Service as the driving value of my career.

I've heard many other leaders say the same thing. And I do see examples in the world of incredible servant leadership.

However, I also see confusion between *service* and *self-sacrifice*. In fact, I used to be confused on that myself. I told myself that "the hustle" came before everything else: sleep, meals, rest.

With the help of my tribe, I came to understand that sacrificing myself for the greater good wasn't service. It was martyrdom.

I also saw that it set an example for the people I led, the very people I wanted to serve, that *they* should also sacrifice themselves in order to serve. Wrong.

It took a lot of reflection to come to the understanding of service that I hold today. Service isn't just constant productivity, nor is it meeting everyone else's needs before your own. True service boils down to something simpler.

Listening.

So often, I see people in positions of leadership who claim to want to serve, but believe they already know exactly what people need. Many times, they've made a decision on what people need without asking questions or seeking to understand the people they claim to serve.

Blind service isn't service. Service arises from listening to people, without judgment, without prejudice. Let them speak for themselves. Listen to what they have to say.

The reason I hold Service as one of my core leadership values is that I've seen how truly listening to people is often what makes them feel safe, welcomed, and valued. As a leader, one of my primary responsibilities is to create an environment where people feel safe enough to take full accountability—to fully own their work, their decisions, their behavior, their successes, their mistakes.

I can't know what that looks like unless I listen. So that's where service starts for me. I want to hear what people have to say in their own words. I want to hear people speak for themselves.

ACCOUNTABILITY

Creating an environment where people feel safe enough to take accountability begins with me. If I'm not accountable to my tribe, my community, my family, and myself, how can I expect anyone else to be?

If I had to name the one value I see *least* represented in our current business environment, it's Accountability. Everywhere I look these days, I see people pointing the finger away from themselves. Very rarely do I see examples of people owning their actions, their mistakes, their words. I see a culture of blame, rather than a culture of accountability.

One thing that was consistent in my childhood was being victimized. So often through what I faced, I was in the role of the victim. And what that gave me was something very different from *victimhood*. When I was a child placed in situations I couldn't own or control, the vow I made myself was to build a life where that could *never* happen again. Where I would never be the victim—of people or of circumstance.

I decided at a young age that to truly control everything that happened to me, I had to take responsibility for everything that happened to me. I believe that's where my accountability drive truly began.

That said, accountability doesn't look like taking responsibility for *other people*, for their actions or deeds. In fact, in a way, that takes away their own control. I don't hold others accountable—that's up to them to hold themselves accountable, not me—but I also don't carry their water for them. That doesn't serve them.

Accountability is a truly beautiful thing. It feels to me almost like a relief. I remember when I was younger thinking, *Wait, if I take ownership of everything in my life… that means I get to control everything that happens to me! That means nobody controls me, but me.*

This is a mindset I often see missing in today's society. I see it everywhere, in every generation, every demographic, every industry. People always looking to point at external reasons why they couldn't do something or get somewhere. Or people throwing out excuses for why they didn't live up to their word, achieve something they set out to do. People not owning their mistakes.

I published an article a while back asking why more leaders don't share their mistakes. Everywhere you look in business media, you see headlines like, "The Top Ten Ways I Built An Eight-Figure Business." "The Five Wins that Made Me A Success."

How about, "The Top Five Biggest Mistakes I've Ever Made"? As a leader, one of the greatest acts of service is to share your mistakes. Show people what it looks like to own them. Take accountability for things you'd do differently. Model a better way of approaching common problems—by giving insight into all the problems you *didn't* solve.

When I decide to make a change in my life, there's only one person who's going to make it happen: me. There's also only one person who's going to derail it: me. I fully own the direction I choose to move in.

I've heard, "Well, not everyone's like you. Not everyone can just decide to change, and then change."

Why not? What's stopping you?

If you're listing things in your head besides yourself, it's time to reflect on accountability and what it means to you.

When I was a kid, if I wasn't confident, or at least didn't come off as confident, I'd be in a very bad position. Where I was from, people smell fear. Confidence was sometimes the only difference between safety and danger. I chose back then to control what I could control. I chose to wake up and be confident, because that was all I had. Confidence is free.

Starting in my twenties, I built wealth from zero dollars to several million. I did it all on my own, by watching, listening, and teaching myself how to trade stocks and be strategic with my finances. Then, when I was wealthier than I ever could have imagined as a hungry child or a homeless teen, I lost it all. I went broke. I had to borrow money just to survive.

It happened because I was missing key insights that if I'd been raised with money, brought up in the playbook, I already would have known. I would have been taught what mistakes to avoid.

I would have had the network and relationships to prevent disaster. It would have been easy for me to point the finger at the playbook. It would have been easy for me to blame my circumstances.

But I can't control the playbook. I can't control the circumstances I was born into. I can't control the hand of cards I was dealt. All I can control is how I play it. Every decision I make is mine, no one else's.

Circumstance isn't making my decisions. I am.

There's a lot in this world you can't control. Why not make it your mission to control what you can?

BE YOUR OWN LEADER

If you've read this chapter and plan to follow it as a guide, don't.

I don't want you to.

What you just read is my code, not yours. One singular playbook followed by every leader is how we wound up with a broken system that leaves most people out.

Leadership is inclusivity. Leadership is welcoming. Leadership is decision-making—but not speaking *for* others. It's listening, learning, and seeking to understand. The Modern Leader makes it their mission to find the barriers to entry that the old playbook created and tear them down one by one. The Modern Leader's mission is to open their eyes, open doors, and open a backpack. Create an environment where everyone—*all people*—can take control of their destiny, and create a future together.

Opportunity is not a zero sum game. We can all rise together.

Maybe the old playbook got you this far. Maybe it's been the primary architect of the world you inhabit. That's not your fault. But it is your responsibility. You own what happens next.

If you're still holding on to the old playbook, I invite you to let it go. Step forward and leave it behind.

My Modern Leader code isn't the same as yours, so now is the time to discover what drives you. What is your code? What values will you be accountable to?

Your first responsibility as a Modern Leader is to ask yourself questions, listen to the answers, and define those values for yourself. They may not look like the past. They may not look like mine. They will look like yours, and that's what's important.

Throw away the playbook.

It's time to stop following. It's time to lead.

CONCLUSION

HOW WE'LL
GET THERE

I RECLAIMED MY NAME IN A MOMENT OF FRUSTRATION, exhaustion, and sorrow.

It was hard to feel any positivity in the summer of 2020. Finding the optimism that had guided me throughout my entire life and career was a challenge.

But I did find some, and it came from an unlikely place. In Scribe's largest conference room, we have a library of every book the company has helped publish. My book, *I Got There*, has its own small section on the shelves, the spines emblazoned with "JT McCormick".

The cover of the book features a photo of me as a little kid, six or seven years old. In the photo, I'm smiling, and even though by that age I'd seen and been through some hair-raising chaos, I still look cheerful. I look excited about what's to come.

The boy on the cover of that book was JeVon. Looking at it in the summer of 2020, I found my glimmer of optimism. I could do something for that little boy, and I could do something for countless other kids looking to their future. I could take back the name my mom gave me. JeVon McCormick. I could show the little JeVons of the world that they belonged in rooms they could barely imagine, let alone see themselves in.

I say "take back", but I'll be honest. No one took that name from me. I made the decision to put it aside. I made the decision to edit myself to fit the old playbook. I made myself part of the problem.

It was my choice to put it down, and it was my responsibility to pick it back up.

I had a responsibility as a Modern Leader to everyone whose eyes might be opened. I had a responsibility to hold open the door for all the JeVons coming in behind me.

Most of all, I had a responsibility to myself.

I'm grateful to the twenty-three-year-old JeVon who decided to put down his name in order to build the life of my dreams. And I'm grateful I got the chance, all these years later, to pay him back for that sacrifice.

LIVING AS JEVON

Seeing my name in lights for the first time was a humbling experience.

Sure, I'd seen JT McCormick on the programs of dozens of conferences, splashed across screens before many a keynote. JT McCormick knew his way around a stage. The audience knew what to expect from him.

They'd never met JeVon. How would they react to him?

I was about to find out. I stood backstage at the largest event I'd ever been asked to appear at, a conference with thousands in attendance. An audience of, specifically, those in the legal profession. You couldn't have dreamed up a more old-playbook crowd. JT McCormick was a name that didn't turn a single head, whereas I was relatively certain JeVon was a name none of them had encountered before in their lives.

Waiting in the dark wings of the large conference hall, I heard the audience fall quiet as the house lights lowered. From the state of the art sound system, I heard my own voice echo. Clips of past JT McCormick keynotes flashed on the huge LED screens that lined the back of the stage. As introductions went, this sizzle reel was like a sonic boom; I felt like I was watching a trailer for a movie about myself, and the movie looked like a hit.

Suddenly, there it was: my name. The huge bright letters spelling *JEVON MCCORMICK* were the only lights in the entire auditorium.

In its glow, I could see the faces of the audience. I didn't see any confusion there. My name, my real name, was headlining this event, and the audience's reaction was curiosity and excitement. Any nerves I'd had jangling around in my chest left me. JeVon was about to step out onstage for the first time, and I had reason to believe he would be met with a warm welcome.

Before I took that step, I remembered something my mom always used to say about life.

This isn't a dress rehearsal.

We only get one shot at this. Life has no second takes. Every moment is the real thing, and every moment is one we won't see come again.

I felt relief that day knowing that all the rest of my moments would be lived as JeVon.

THIRTEEN WORDS

When I was in the final stages of writing this book, I had to pause to go through the hardest moment of my life so far. My mom passed away. The three weeks I spent saying goodbye and then moving through the aftermath are a time I find difficult to remember, but that I'll never forget.

My mom and I were close. After all, we went through my childhood together—we *survived* it together. During most of those years, we didn't have money, we often didn't have food, and sometimes we didn't even have water or electricity. But we had each other.

Home was wherever me and my mom were together, and she made sure that home was full of love, even if it was empty of nearly everything else.

Even as close as I was to her, I know there were things about her life that my mom never shared with me. There are parts of her story I'll never hear.

When she passed, I learned this firsthand. I discovered something about her I had never known.

My mother, Anna Marie McCormick, was an incredibly talented writer.

She was raised in an orphanage. When she was 18, she was turned out on the streets with the borrowed name McCormick, a tattered blue suitcase, and little else. She became a single mom not long after and spent decades trying to protect me, her only child, from the cruelty of the world that surrounded us. Shielding me from the taunts we received because I was mixed race. Working every minute of the day to try to keep us fed, keep a roof over our heads.

I sat next to my mom on the curb as a child and watched her

cry when we were evicted. I held the hospital bill from my birth in my hands and saw the "Welf" next to her name that marked her as a welfare mother. I know the pain and struggle that punctuated her years on this earth. I experienced much of her story with her, but there are untold pieces of her past that even I will never know. No one will ever know.

But they could have.

Because my mother was an amazing writer, and no one ever knew that. She was more than capable of telling her own story, but she never had the opportunity.

After she was gone, I received an envelope she had left for me. In it was a simple note.

Son, now that my time has passed, when I look back on my life, I know my only accomplishment in life was that I had you. This is in honor of you, Son, and all that you have accomplished in book publishing.

There was another sheet of paper, and on it, she had written her own obituary. Here is what she wrote.

I, Anna Marie (McCormick) Stark turned the last page in the book of my life on March 23, 2022.

Some chapters are glorious, some hold deep sorrows and disappointments.

Many times I do not want to finish my book at all.

However, as I write the last chapter, it is filled with deepest gratitude, unparalleled love, joy, and peace.

My son JeVon Thomas McCormick, my daughter in law Megan Ann, and my four grandchildren, Ava Ann, Jaxon Thomas, Elle Marie, and Jace Thomas, as well as my husband, E.J. Stark, will know my love for them is unceasing.

Everyone has a story, so as it should be, I leave with nothing unsaid, no chapters unread.

Please do not judge my story by the chapter you walked in on.

Today I closed my book.

It's impossible to express what I felt when I read this final message from her. I'll never be able to put it into words.

I love my mom. I miss her. She and I were the only two people who shared an experience that, even filled with deep sorrows and disappointments, was also extraordinary in its own way. We shared a name that has no past, and now has a future in my own children. We shared a time and a place that made me the man I am.

Please do not judge my story by the chapter you walked in on. How did she manage to tell such a heartbreaking story, the story of a lifetime, in just thirteen words?

The world's eyes were never opened to her talent. I want nothing more than to read more of her writing, but there will be no more. That was all she wrote.

A NEW STORY

I think often about all the doors that were closed to my mom before she got anywhere near them. I think about all the roads she could have walked down in her life that she didn't even know existed. No one opened her eyes to what was possible. I think about how she entered this world with none of the supplies she would need to survive. How she scraped and struggled to fill her own backpack, and then took supplies out of her backpack to fill mine.

What might my mom have seen if her eyes had been opened? What more might she have been able to do, had she been welcomed through an open door?

There are stories in this world that deserve to be told. There are voices that deserve to be heard.

I believe that, despite everything, the world is ready to listen.

We're ready to hear a new story.

As a Modern Leader, it's my responsibility to help bring those stories into the light. To not only make space, but to welcome them to the forefront of the conversation.

Because the conversation has been incomplete. It's been missing crucial perspectives, critical insights, that create a more complete picture of our future. It was missing my story, until I learned how to edit it.

I learned to put people first by watching a pimp collect money from prostitutes. I learned to see what was possible by driving through the wealthiest neighborhood in Houston. I learned to empower people to thrive in their opportunities by seeing a kid's backpack full of the supplies he needed to succeed in school. I've built businesses that flourish by making people the foundation of every decision.

I got there. I did it on my own. I had to leave behind my past, my story, and my name. But that wasn't Modern Leadership.

Modern Leadership doesn't leave anyone behind.

That's how I got there, but that's not our future. A new story is being written by voices that now get to be heard for the first time. If those of us who have already been heard have any privilege, it's that we get to simply listen.

The future of business won't look anything like its past. There is no playbook that will tell us how to win the decades to come. The work we have to do together is challenging, and it's not a game.

But we will do the work. We'll do it with optimism and accountability. We'll do it by asking questions and listening to each other's stories. We'll do it with eyes, doors, minds, and hearts open.

That's how we'll get there.

Together.

ACKNOWLEDGMENTS

FOR ME, LEADERSHIP LESSONS CAME FROM THE MOST unexpected places. As such, I have endless appreciation and love for my parents Anna Marie McCormick and William "Boobie" Cochran. Both directly and indirectly, the two of you taught me how to survive. More importantly, you gave me life. Thank You for the intense chaos, and for exposing me to an environment the majority of America will never know, and Damn sure never understand.

To my Wife-Queen Megan Ann McCormick. You have had a front-row seat to watch me teach and lead myself on how to have a healthy relationship, and as you well know, you are my first, my last, and my everything. Thank You for always standing by my side.

To Ava Ann McCormick, Jaxon Thomas McCormick, Elle Marie McCormick, and Jace Thomas McCormick. I believe one day you will read this book, and my only request is that each of you NEVER say, "I want to be like my dad". If there is anything that you appreciate about me, instead say to yourself, "I want to be a billion times better than my dad". Don't be like me, or anyone else; be the greatest *you*, and above all, love yourself first. Never forget, a positive attitude changes everything, always take responsibility and accountability for your actions, and life is nothing more than choices. Choose wisely, and always know that Daddy loves you unconditionally, even when you make mistakes.

I only have five friends. I know a lot of people, but I only have five friends. Three of those friends are Tucker Max, Brittany Claudius, and Meghan McCracken. As you all know, my vocabulary is limited, so I truly do not have the words to express my sincere appreciation for all your loyalty, trust, and friendship. Thank You for your belief in me, and for allowing me to lead.

Tucker, no matter how long I live, you Sir gave me one of the greatest gifts I've ever received. You told me that "I was the fastest learner you'd ever met". Truly life changing. Thank You!

Meghan aka "The Cracken", Thank You for serving as my translator, capturing my voice, and always understanding what I'm "saying" even when I don't have the words.

Scribe Media, the Scribe Tribe! As each of you have heard me say countless times, I'm only as good as the GREAT people I get to serve and support. Scribe Media is everything that it is because of each of you. Thank You for allowing me to lead.

God, back when I was thirteen years old, homeless, by myself on a bus stop, with no money, no food, and no place to go, only You could have known I'd have the life I have now. Thank You for my gifts, talents, blessings, and my amazing life. I may be a Modern Leader, but I will only, and always, follow You.

"Everyone has a story, so never judge anyone, because you don't know their story."

—ANNA MARIE MCCORMICK

ABOUT THE AUTHOR

JeVon McCormick is the President and CEO of Scribe Media, a publishing company that helps individuals from a variety of backgrounds write, publish, and market their books. Recently named Best CEO in Austin, TX, JeVon is also an author and highly sought-after keynote speaker, delivering the message that "Everyone Has A Story" to enthusiastic audiences across the country. JeVon is passionate about conscious entrepreneurship and creating opportunities for at-risk youth. He has mentored young men and women in the juvenile justice system, as well as those in lower economic communities.

JeVon currently serves as a board member for Conscious Capitalism and the StartEdUp Foundation. His story and work have been featured on CNBC, and in Entrepreneur, Forbes, and Inc. magazines. He lives in Austin with his wife, Megan, and their four children Ava, Jaxon, Elle, and Jace.

CPSIA information can be obtained
at www.ICGtesting.com
Printed in the USA
LVHW041639040423
743434LV00016B/531/J

9 781544 532288